THE ROUND TABLE

*How to Leverage the Skills of Multiple
Professions to Revitalize a Situation*

Abraham M. Gutsioglou, Ph.D.

Published by Think Differently LLC
www.thinkdiff-llc.com

The Round Table Copyright © 2019 by Abraham M. Gutsioglou

ISBN: 9781080869459

DEDICATION

To my wife who has been my support system, my coach, my consultant, my sounding board – the list goes on. Thank you for inspiring me to do more, to challenge myself, and to help all the people we can along the way!

CONTENTS

ACKNOWLEDGMENTS

Many people have inspired the evolution of this book. My respect and appreciation have grown immensely for all of you (the professionals) who have expanded my understanding of the world and the problems that surround our every-day lives. You have helped me to see the world in a different way, you have helped me to Think Differently. Special thanks to Hagi Fuentes for the late nights of work, creative thinking, and the insights we have gained along the way.

Thank you!

INTRODUCTION

This book is inspired by tactics, techniques, and mindsets to turn things around when everything is going wrong!

I wrote this book because there are tons of academic books, consultant guides, and endless PowerPoints on how to implement business transformations, but most of them approach the topic through the lens of projects running smoothly– in a straight line. I don't know about you, but I have yet to see a business transformation that follows a perfectly linear path. So, I decided to put my thoughts on paper to create a less traditional guide for creating business transformations and ways to recover for when things start to fall-apart.

The idea to write this book came to me while I was on a business trip, sitting alone in a hotel restaurant thousands of miles away from my family and home. As I sat there eating (what felt like a cold hamburger) feeling frustrated and deflated by the day's work, I questioned my existence. I allowed my mind to wander and quickly found myself in deep reflection. The more I mentally let go, the more my natural surroundings heightened. I sat there watching how the people around me interacted, what they said to each other, how they behaved toward one-another (mainly, stimulus – response type of interactions it seemed) – and then it hit me! All of these people are "acting"– playing a role within their environment, or flashing a persona, so to speak. Thinking like a psychologist, I began to explore the patterns and various personalities at play. It was at this point that I flipped things inwardly, and reflected on how I showed up in the workplace, on projects that went well, projects that were a mess. I realized that when things were going bad, I found myself embodying a specific persona – one that applied key tactics to help turn things around. I began thinking about as many shitty situations as I could remember from various projects, and mapped them onto the mindset that I had (up to that point-subconsciously) been using to help get me through various trials and tribulations. On that very same napkin I wrote down a model that I created to help me work through business and personal challenges.

As a result of that evening you get this book. It is written in two parts. Part One: shows you the transformation model—here, I will guide you through what each of its elements represent, and provide you with insight on how and when to use it. Part Two: explores various personas you can leverage to help you revitalize a struggling situation. Each chapter represents a profession (i.e. persona), which I characterized by a particular set of problems/challenges, tactics, techniques and views of the world that can be applied to any number of scenarios.

This book is meant to be a companion on your journey, to help ensure things are in your favor and under control as much as possible. Although it is written as a guide to be added to your professional toolkit, I have also found that many of the concepts apply to everyday life. I encourage you to apply and expand the many things you learn from this book. I hope that you find the ideas I am sharing with you useful.

Thank you for coming along with me on this journey.

PART ONE

☺ SAY HELLO TO THE TRANSFORMATION MODEL ☺

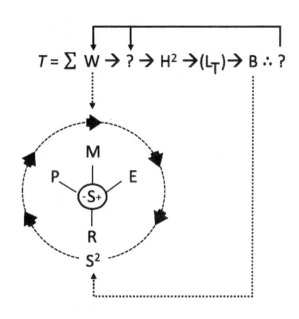

THE TRANSFORMATION MODEL
THE KEYS TO UNDERSTANDING THE ELEMENTS

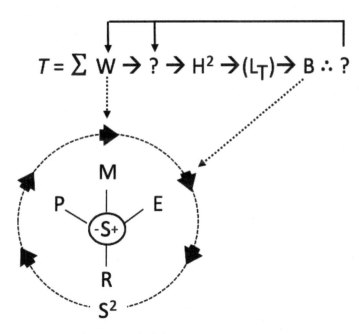

Figure 1.1: The Transformation Model

Let's start by breaking down each element of the transformation model. Trust me, it looks much more complicated than it really is.

Once you understand the elements and use it a handful of times you won't have to refer back to it, because it will become a natural part of your approach. After going through the model, we will close off the chapter by putting it all together, so that you get a better idea of how to apply the model.

T stands for "transformation." It's that simple.

Σ represents the summation of your entire approach and work effort.

> Basically, everything you do will add up to help you create the transformation. I am in the process of converting this model into an actual formula with numerical weights, but you don't need to worry about a formula for now – that is something that will come out in a future publication. For now, just leverage the elements.

W stands for "what do you want?"

> It can be something like, implementing a new business process or launching a new technology that people must adopt. Remember, it can also apply to a personal goal like making a career move, learning a new skill, or embracing kindness. Yep, kindness.

$?$ stands for "why do you want this?"

> Having a clear reason as to why you want your "what" will take you a long way. When things get tough (and they will)

your "why" is your North Star – you need to come back to it often to remind yourself why you want this. If you are approaching a problem as the fixer, "why" should be your first target of focus. Understanding this element will help you get things back in order. It is also what you will use to get others tethered to your momentum.

H^2 stands for "How will you know you have it (or getting close)?" and "How are you keeping track?" It is squared because there are two H's in the model.

The first piece reminds you that you need to be clear on your objective, while the second piece forces you to put a gauge in place. For example, as a fixer, how will you know things are getting better? Are team members barking at each other less? If so, how are you measuring that? Will staff be more aware of your campaign? If yes, how do you know more people actually know it exists – are they talking about it, are they asking more questions? If you are working on a personal transformation, ask yourself...Am I less stressed? Am I meeting new people or making new friends? You get the idea; you need a clear objective with a clear and tangible measurement.

LT stands for "Length of Time."

This element of the model will make things much more complicated – or more fun, for you depending on your view of the world. It will inform how (un)realistic your transformational goal is. It is important that you don't fall into the trap of thinking more time means higher chance of being successful. I have found that having too much time is just as bad as having very little or no-time. You will find that when time is slipping away and you have very little of it left on a project, more things will start to fall-apart. When things go haywire, people freak-out and let their emotions get the best of them. However, when you are brought in to fix a situation, your job is to "stop time", meaning you assess the situation, and begin pulling on the levers in the model to stabilize it. The less time you have the harder and more aggressive your tactics need to be. Stay focused.

B stands for "Barriers or Blockers" that <u>**will**</u> get in your way.

Allow me to strongly emphasize the point that there will be things that will get in the way. Just when you think things are turning around, you can count on something new to arise that makes sure your plan begins to deviate. It's life! Don't get discouraged, just rely on your wealth of previous experience to inform the future. If you don't feel like you have the experience, that's okay too, because you can use the experience of others in the situation. In the model, this part connects with S^2 (keep reading ☺). As a heads-up, two of the most common things you can count on to get in your way are people (emotions, behaviors, patterns) and processes (ways of doing things or not doing them).

Physical - Mental – Emotional levers you need to pull and apply a negative, neutral, or positive Stimulus to obtain a specific outcome (Response). The outcome will inform you how much you need to adjust your strategy. We will see some ideas in detail when we bring the entire model together into a few situations. This piece of the model connects to the professions in Part Two of the book.

S² stands for "Support System."

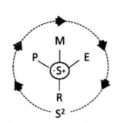

Figure 1.2: The Support System

As you begin to make adjustments and turning the situation around, you will need a system to help you reinforce the changes you have applied. I see this as a person or group of people put in place to keep the momentum going long after you are gone. It can also be a place/environment that is put in place or adjusted to remind people to stay focused and on track. A support system can also be a thing, a symbolic reminder (e.g., a logo, crest, brand, mascot, etc.). A support system is the equivalent of training wheels or guardrails, because they are meant to keep you going on a path. Just like training wheels, a support system is also temporary – you need it long enough to build confidence, trust, and behavioral patterns (i.e., predictable behaviors in ways of working).

∴ stands for "Therefore."

In the context of this model it represents the philosophical question of "Now What?" Once you have reached your goals, turned things around, or at least started to near the end-game, you need to ask yourself things like, now what? Do I need to rinse and repeat or should I refresh my methodology or approach and (re)execute? The answer will depend on the whole reason you are pursuing the goal in the first place. If you were called to fix a situation and you fixed it – that's it you're done. If it was tied to a personal goal, you'll need to reflect on this element a bit longer, as it may indicate you have more work to do.

THE TRANSFORMATION MODEL: BRINGING IT ALL TOGETHER

Projects go south for many reasons. They can deteriorate because of unresolved or hidden problems, the project keeps getting stalled, the initiative has a bad reputation, and so on – we can be here a while. Sometimes you are directly involved and you can see the failure coming, while other times, you are doing your own thing and suddenly get invited to the party. In this section, a scenario is presented and use the model in the form of patterned questions to bring it all together.

THE CLIENT:

Your client has an aggressive strategic plan to expand its portfolio of services and goods. To do this, the company needs to grow its portfolio through acquisitions. The company has been doing this for years and is good at powering through financial research, negotiations, and legal. However, they failed to consider that new acquisitions come with personalities filled with emotions, hopes, and dreams – oh yeah, and baggage. The client believes that leaving the newly acquired companies alone (as if nothing ever happened) means that they would keep performing. Their philosophy is, "If we don't disturb them, nothing will happen." The problem with this philosophy is that it rarely works. You (the consultant) get called in because several of the previously acquired companies have started to act out, underperform, or express feelings of distrust for "corporate." Your task is to put a strategy in place to turn this around. The client has no plans of slowing down, so they need you to help them sort this out, like yesterday (as they say)!

THE TRANSFORMATION MODEL IN ACTION:

As a "fixer" you'll need to have an intake conversation with the main person of interest, likely the executive sponsor who has a vested interest in things actually turning around. If you fail to have the conversation with the right person, you're wasting your time. Let's go with the assumption that you have the right person.

Applying the model is as simple as getting the answers to these questions from the client.

1. What do you want to accomplish?
2. Why do you want this / why is this important?
3. How will you know we have accomplished this goal (what's the measure)?
4. How much time do we have?
5. What are things that will get in the way?
6. Are you willing to do what I ask of you and to provide the needed support to get this done?

Here's a simplified conversation between you and the client.

Note, real conversations will be more complicated, the client may not provide clear answers or just put the entire weight of solving the problem on your shoulders. Over time you will get good at navigating these types of conversations and getting all the details you need to move forward.

YOU: What do you want to accomplish?

> **CLIENT**: I need company X employees to stop bad mouthing headquarters, I need company Y to stop fighting and sabotaging us as we try to integrate their systems to ours, and finally, I need company Z employees to include others on the deals they are working on. They just all need to get along with us.

YOU: Why do you want this / why is this important?

> **CLIENT:** If they don't get along with us or become inclusive, we can't sell or hit the market the way we planned.

YOU: How will you know we have accomplished this goal (what's the measure)?

> **CLIENT:** Well, to start people will stop bad-mouthing each other, we will actually show-up to clients as a unified front, and we will win the deals. Our deal win-rates should be increasing not staying flat.

YOU: How much time do we have?

> **CLIENT:** YESTERDAY! We will keep expanding our portfolio and I don't have time to babysit them because they don't get along.

YOU: What are things that will get in the way?

> **CLIENT:** I feel like the middle level management and some of the executives will make it hard for you to get this going. They have egos and pride that stops them from creating synergies.

YOU: I will need you to do things or be places. In fact, this will cost you: time, money, resources (things and people), and maybe even your reputation. Are you willing to do what is needed to get this done?

CLIENT: YES! (Note, be cautious here, they often say yes, but when things get worse, they will transfer the pressure over to you).

Chapter One

Summary

In this chapter, you learned that projects go on a declining path and fail for many reasons; most of them fall apart because of people related problems. You can expect to see things like: unresolved conflicts, hidden agendas, insecurities, fears, and so on.

There will be times when you are part of a project in the early phases and you will see first-hand where the issue comes from, then other times, when you are going to be brought in as an outsider to turn things around.

As a "fixer" it is helpful to have a model to work with, something to get you thinking about key elements to leverage through the process. This chapter introduced you to the Transformation Model, a mental model that guides you through a process of getting failing situations back on track.

Applying the model is as simple as getting the answers to these questions:

1. What do you want to accomplish?
2. Why do you want this / why is this important?
3. How will you know we have accomplished this goal (what's the measure)?
4. How much time do we have?
5. What are things that will get in the way?

6. Are you willing to do what I ask of you, and provide the support needed to get this done?

As you learn to use the model, you will also learn to challenge your way of thinking by seeing the world through the lens of different professions. Over the course of a single project you will need to leverage the thinking skills of professions (or personas) other than your own.

The rest of this book will introduce you to various professions and ways of thinking, so that you can revitalize a failing situation.

PART TWO
MEET THE PROFESSIONALS

ARE YOU IN A FAILING PROJECT OR SITUATION?
THE ROUND TABLE

Imagine this - a challenge has presented itself where your client needs a fixer. They need you to help them turn things around. Visualize yourself sitting at the round table, a place where all perspectives are respected and professions are treated as peers. As you sit there being your calm, cool, and collected self, you take a subtle deep breath. Then, you glance toward your left-hand side to see the psychologist you interact with when you need psychological expertise; then, as you move your way clockwise, you make eye-contact with your investigator, researcher, diagnostician, air traffic controller, campaign strategist, and lawyer.

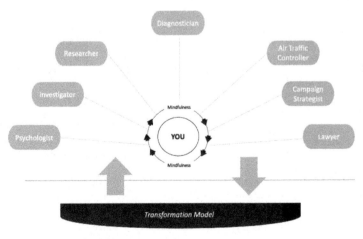

Figure 1-3: The round table

All of these individuals are within reach day and night, any day of the year, all of them there to assist you as the need arises. There will be times when a problem presents itself and you will need to leverage the skills, talents, and expertise of every single one of them. Other times, you will be presented with challenges when you don't need them all, instead you need a subset, or perhaps the skills of just one of them – whichever way you need it, you have it. Nice. Isn't it?

Let's bring you back to reality. Most of us don't have the luxury of having a staff like this at our fingertips; especially, if you are running your own small consultancy practice. This part of the book is designed to provide you with insights into each of these professions, so that you have a basic understanding of their ways of working and– perhaps– learn a thing or two that you can integrate into your own turnaround strategies. Advancing through each chapter will help you unlock new lessons and different ways of thinking based on a particular profession's persona. You are at the center of it all, along with the mindfulness aura you radiate. Beneath the surface is your subconscious in which the transformation model (from the first part of this book) lives. As you move through daily interactions you will dip in/out of the model, taking key elements you need to create strategies to revitalize failing situations.

THE MINDFUL CONSULTANT
PUT YOUR OXYGEN MASK ON FIRST

"Between stimulus and response there is a space. In that space is our power to choose our response. In our response lies our growth and our freedom." ~ Viktor Frankl

Think of the last time you boarded an airplane: if you are like me and most people, you settled into your seat, adjusted the vent temperature, untangled your headphones, pulled out your eye-mask, plugged in your favorite electronic device to charge, and ran one last social media/email check. As you waited for the crew to run through their standard operating procedures, you also likely ignored the safety presentation. It seems many people ignore it because they trust an emergency won't occur, or because they already "know" the procedure. I am here to remind you of one of the most important elements of that safety presentation – the oxygen mask procedure. To quote the many wise and friendly airline attendants – **"Please,**

put your oxygen mask on first before assisting others – because if you die in the process of putting theirs on first, then they die, you die, and we all die." I added that last part for emphasis– I have a feeling that it won't catch on or be added to the next safety video.

The Mindfulness Perspective	
Common areas to apply this perspective	• Organizational designs (restructures, workforce reductions) • Disruptive team interventions • Leadership retreats
Qualities of practicing mindfulness	• Observing the world in a non-judgmental way • Impartial focus and attention • In the moment awareness

Table 2-1: The mindfulness perspective

WHY MINDFULNESS?

What does an oxygen mask have to do with mindfulness or helping clients anyway? Well, before you can help others turn things around, you need to start by having your house in order. This part of the book is strictly focused on you. Your goal should be to have a mind that is calm, cool, collected, and ready for prime-time. This should be a critical focus of your practice because your clients will be able to read your thoughts – okay, maybe not actually read them, but they will be able to see how you respond to sticky situations. The more often you are exposed to highly stressful and anxiety charged situations, the more tools you need at your disposal to help you through them.

WHAT'S MINDFULNESS ANYWAY?

There are many definitions of mindfulness, but there is one definition I find to be very clear, meaningful, and simple for busy consultants like you and me to understand. It comes from an expert in the field, a long-time student of Zen, Yoga, and creator of the Stress Reduction Clinic (among many other great accomplishments) Jon Kabat-Zinn.

"Mindfulness means paying attention in a particular way: on purpose, in the present moment and non-judgmentally."[1]

~ *Jon Kabat-Zinn* ~

If there is one thing for certain, it's that people will project their insecurities, fears, feelings, and desires onto you - we do this to others, so you are not exempt from this (more on projections in Chapter 3). The practice of mindfulness comes with many benefits, a key among them being to help you be better at identifying when, where, how, and why you and the client experience stress. Even better, mindfulness enables you to adapt yourself and adjust your emotions without (or at least, with minimal) judgement throughout the process.

TECHNIQUE #1 – KEEP IT SIMPLE: START BY BREATHING

Okay, how do you pay attention to the current moment, on purpose, and without attaching judgement to it – without being a meditation guru? The answer is so simple and basic that you will question its effectiveness. All you have to do is – breathe! Yes, it's that simple. According to Chade-Meng Tan, author of *Search Inside Yourself: The Unexpected Path to Achieving Success, Happiness (and World Peace)*[2], in order for you to be able to focus on what's happening out in the world you need to focus on what is happening inside yourself. Don't overthink practicing mindfulness, just start by breathing. Don't worry about the chaos yet–it will be there waiting for you, the difference is that after controlling your breathing, you will be able to navigate through it with a focused mind. There is a saying out in the mindfulness community that goes…

"you can't stop the waves, but you can learn to surf."

Try this out: it is my interpretation of applying mindfulness in three minutes.

Do This	What It Does
Step 1: Find a quiet place where you can be alone (sit, stand or lay down).	This helps you to begin paying attention on purpose.
Step 2: Close your eyes, take a deep breath, let it go.	This helps you to focus on the current moment and nothing else.
Step 3: Repeat this for three minutes. The key is to only focus on a single breath at a time, nothing more, nothing less.	This helps you to stay between the past and the future without casting judgement.

Table 2-2: Three-minute mindfulness

Now that you have mastered breath-control, we can move on to sharpening your focus. The next two techniques I am going to share with you I learned by interviewing therapists and researching stress reduction techniques. If you are interested in learning more, reach out to a licensed professional.

TECHNIQUE #2 – SHARPEN YOUR FOCUS BY TURNING AUTOPILOT OFF

We spend the majority of our day responding to stimuli across our environment. Client emails (stimulus), we email back promptly (response). Client calls (stimulus), we answer (response). Client needs to change scope (stimulus), we freak out and adjust accordingly (response) – you get the point. This cyclical pattern is what I refer to as our autopilot feature. Learning to turn-off your cognitive autopilot will help you to pay attention to the details of objects, events, people, and overall senses. One technique to help you master this skill is called the "raisin exercise." Though a raisin is the classic object used in this activity, you can actually use any other object of your choice; the essence of the exercise is simply to help you bring curiosity and intentional focus within your control. Again, the goal is for you to turn-off your autopilot feature and pay attention to what's in front of you, one breath at a time.

Let's give it a try for three minutes.

Minute one: Focus on your breath. Calm your thoughts.

Minute two: Take the object of your choice (make sure it is not an electronic device that will distract you) in your hands, pretend like you have never seen this object before, examine every part of it. Simply pay attention to the lines, details, colors, texture, etc. To help keep your mind focused on the task, try narrating the details of the object in your mind. For example, you can say to yourself, this object is blue, it has lines, the object is round, etc.

Minute three: Put the object down and away. Close your eyes. Bring your focus back to your breath. Calm your thoughts. Open your eyes. Welcome back to your day.

As you mature your practice of attention, you will be able to expand the timeframe. Your goal should be to expand this practice into your world with clients, in which, you don't need to close your eyes – instead, you are in the moment paying attention to details of what they say, how they behave (verbal and non-verbal), and how others respond to the situation you are in.

TECHNIQUE #3 – EXPAND YOUR PERCEPTION THROUGH BODY SCANNING

Look at you! Living in the moment, paying attention to details, what's next – expanding your perceptions? Actually, yes, that is next. "Body scanning" is a technique used in mindfulness to enhance your ability to notice what is happening inside your body and how that connects to what you are feeling and thinking. Noticing the interconnectedness between your bodily sensations, thoughts, and feelings, in this way will help you paint a vivid picture of yourself and others around you.

> *Try this:* Focus on your breath. Calm your thoughts. Pay attention to how your body feels from the inside, start with the top of your head and scan your sensations down to your toes. Depending on your position you will feel aches, pains, tension and so on. Just feel them acknowledge they are there and let them be. The idea here is that you are noticing what is happening without trying to control it.

As your attention to detail evolves, so will your ability to identify what is a contributing factor to how you feel. All of this becomes helpful to protect you from the negativity that will be thrown your way – guaranteed! Clients will react with emotions and you my friend will likely be the target. You can expect to hear things like – "I thought you were the expert here, why are we not seeing any immediate results." Just stay focused on the outcome and practice mindfulness to help you keep your perspective under control. Remember, put your oxygen on mask first, before helping anyone.

TECHNIQUE #4 – STOP TIME AND LIVE WITHIN THE BRACKETS

When you are brought into a problematic situation, you will always be at a disadvantage because you will never have the full story. No need to worry – all you have to do is to stop time and live within the brackets. What the heck does that mean and how do you do that? Take a look at the image below (Figure 2-1). One of the many things that you can count on is that most human behavior is consistent, pattern-based, and predictable. Think of it this way, we spend the majority of our day thinking about two aspects of our lives: the past or the future. The extent to which we spend ruminating on either side of the spectrum will detail the level of regret (past) or anxiety (future) that we experience throughout the day.

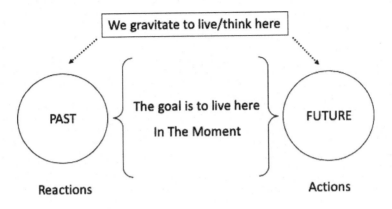

Figure 2-1: Live within the brackets

The average person will use what they know about the past to make speedy calculations and assumptions about the future. Yes, this includes your client. To help your client stay in the moment and process what is happening with the situation at hand, they have to mindfully stop the oscillating effect of past and future mind-frames. This means that you need to spend time coaching them on a one-on-one basis to focus on the present moment and not get hung up on what happened or what's next. Let me remind you, this is much easier said than done. Hang in there. While your client is getting reoriented to the present, you on the other hand need a deeper understanding of the situation that is causing problems for them. The best way to get a richer view and deeper appreciation is for you to do some naturalistic observations. This requires you to study all available behaviors (verbal and non-verbal) in their natural environment without intervening - all you do is observe and take (mental) notes. We will go deeper into this technique in our researcher chapter.

Chapter Two

Summary

In this chapter, you learned that practicing mindfulness can help you deal with challenging situations. This chapter focused on you and making sure that you have the right mindsets (e.g., staying calm, cool, collected, and ready for prime-time) to deal with difficult clients.

As you advance your practice and sharpen your "fixer" skills, mindfulness should remain a critical focus of your evolution. The more you are exposed to highly stressful and challenging situations, the better you will be at managing through them.

Other benefits of practicing mindfulness include:

- Enhanced levels of self-awareness.
- Clearer objectivity.
- Increased ability to handle emotional roller-coasters.

Remember, you can count on people projecting their insecurities, fears, anxieties, and feelings, onto you. Your mindfulness practice will yield many benefits, one of which is improving your skills at identifying when, where, how, and why you (or your client) experience stress. You will be better at flowing with the moment, with minimal judgement and a clear mind.

THE PSYCHOLOGIST
PAY ATTENTION TO YOUR CLIENT, YOU MIGHT FIND WHAT THEY NEED

"Psychology is much bigger than just medicine, or fixing unhealthy things. It's about education, work, marriage - it's even about sports. What I want to do is see psychologists working to help people build strengths in all these domains." ~ Martin Seligman

What is the first thing you think about when you hear the word "psychologist?" How about "psychotherapist?" Most people imagine a Freudian couch scenario, where a person is laying on a couch freely associating thoughts and feelings as they face away from the therapist. Let's get real, psychology (and therapy, for that matter) has come a long way and shows up in the world in surprising ways. I have found it to show up among friends, when one person had a bad day and is sharing, while the other is attentively and actively listening, ending with one friend saying to the other "Thank you for listening to me, it was very therapeutic." Don't get me wrong, it takes years and thousands of hours of practice to become a professionally licensed therapist. I hate to break it to you, but reading this chapter will not make you a psychologist or a therapist; on the bright side, it will help you to think like one, and learn a few basic techniques you can use to help clients.

The Psychologist Perspective

Common areas to apply this perspective	• Performance management • Change management projects • Organizational assessments
Qualities of people in this field	• Cross-cultural sensitivity • Higher tolerance for change • Interpersonal skills (i.e., relationship builder) • Active listening skills

Table 3-1: The psychologist perspective

WHY SHOULD I THINK LIKE A PSYCHOLOGIST?

As a fixer, you will be called into situations where emotions are running high and the pressure is on from every angle. I am going to drastically simplify this, but much like a therapist, your job is to help clients regain control of their situations by implementing ways to manage through the problematic symptoms. There are (and will be) many different reasons you are pulled into a situation. Here are some very common reasons you will be brought along for the client's journey. Remember, this list is not exhaustive – life will surprise you with much more.

Common problems you will hear from clients...

- My team keeps recycling the same problems/issues.
- My project keeps stalling and will not move forward because of the people.
- People on the team hold grudges, sabotage timelines, withhold information, refuse to hold their end of the project, or just don't get along.
- Stress impacts how my people show up on the project (e.g., confident vs. insecure).
- People just don't get it, they lack clarity in roles, responsibilities, and goals.
- My people are not coachable.
- The team lost meaning and attraction to the "why" of the project.

Table 3-2: Client problems

Just as much as we have a list of potential problems, there is also a list of potential solutions.

Here is where and how you can help clients to...

- Reflect about previous project pitfalls and what nurtured their occurrence.
- Increase awareness to identify recurring pitfalls (or replicating patterns).
- Objectively recognize the differences between feelings, opinions, facts, and learn how to implement micro-corrections along the way to avoid drastic negative shifts.
- Create ways to help individuals navigate through stress more effectively.
- Identify the stimulus that triggers problems and create ways to respond differently.
- Define milestones, goals, and pathways to allow teams to work toward them.

Table 3-3: Ways to help

THE TRANSFORMATION MODEL

For this particular persona, you will leverage three components of the transformation model: what do you want to accomplish, how will you know you have it/how are you keeping track and finally what's the support system in place to keep it going. The transformation model is shown below (Figure 3-1) with the three components in bold letters (W- H^2- S^2).

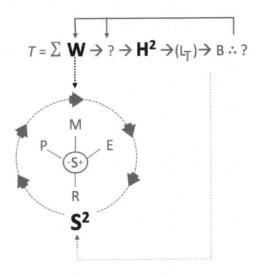

Figure 3-1: The transformation model

As a refresher:

> **W** stands for "what do you want?" - since it is your client who wants a turnaround – the question is rephrased to…what does the client want to accomplish?

> **H²** stands for "How will you know you have it? and "How are you keeping track?" It is squared because there are two H's in the model. Remember, a clear and precise objective is much easier to attain and measure.

> **S²** stands for "Support System" – which becomes critical to the transformation. Creating change is easy, the hard part of change is sustaining it. A support system will help the client reinforce the changes they have made.

TECHNIQUES TO TURN THINGS AROUND

As a consultant in this line of work, you will spend a big portion of your time attending meetings, listening to perspectives, sorting through piles of data, history, background, and generating hypotheses to correct or alleviate problems. By now, you are well aware that you must wear multiple hats and embody various personas to help your client get back on track. The following techniques can be used to channel the skills of your inner psychologist.

TECHNIQUE #1 – LISTEN TO YOUR CLIENT

A major contributor to turning things around is to know what the actual problem is, which can be a time-consuming and complicated process. It is important for you to pay attention to the details and read between the lines (or listen between the lines). More often than not, your client will come to you with symptoms of a problem and not the actual problem. Take for instance, a manager who says *"My team is not getting along, we need teambuilding."* The unexperienced consultant would give them a teambuilding intervention, but not you – you will engage the client in a meaningful conversation. The bottom line is that you will engage them in a conversation where you actively listen, sense their emotions, get the history of the issue at hand, while reading their non-verbal cues to understand the real problem. In the example above, the real problem is rooted in a broken business process that creates communication breakdown among teammates and it shows itself to the manager as the need for a teambuilding activity.

What is "active listening" anyway? According to Carl Rogers (1951) an influential thinker in the field of psychotherapy, active listening is a technique used to create change in a client through communication and feedback. In an interview he defines "active listening" (you can also find the interview on YouTube)[4] as...

"The best kind of listening when you are listening for the feelings and emotions that are behind the words that are just a little bit concealed where you can discern a pattern of feeling behind what was being said"

~ Carl Rogers ~

Try this out next time you are conducting an exploratory/discovery meeting with your client.

Step 1: Pay attention. Most of this meeting will require you to just listen. Sometimes clients run out of things to say or are unable to focus. In the event that happens, you should be prepared with a set of open-ended questions to probe a little bit deeper into the presenting symptoms.

Step 2: Apply active listening. As the client talks, you take notes and ask open-ended questions. Do not lead the client– I repeat, do not lead the client with your questions. Allow the client to express their thoughts, feelings, frustrations, and wishes for the presenting problem.

Step 3: Provide genuine caring feedback. To do this, apply the "mirror" technique, where you paraphrase what the client said. You can say something like this...

"Allow me to share what I heard you say; I want to make sure that I heard you correctly and understand what you are saying to me. If I miss anything please correct me."

Doing this will ensure that you are aligned with your client, you understand their need (at least, the presenting need). This will help you further build the level of trust between you and the client.

Step 4: Stay away from judgement. I can't emphasize this enough: stay away from inserting your personal beliefs about the situation or drawing conclusions from things that you have seen or dealt with in the past. You will be tempted to say things like - "Ah, yes, I have seen this in the past" or "Yep, I totally know what you mean, that's frustrating." There will be plenty of time for you to strategize, compare, and contrast on your own, just don't do it with the client. There are reasons why therapists and coaches do not share their own personal beliefs or judgements, which would take far too long to explain given scope of this book. Trust me on this.

Step 5: Set clear expectations. Some consultants skip this step, but I always do it during the last phase of the contracting conversation. Here's why: first, I need the client to purge the cloudy thoughts they have about the situation; second, I want to come to a better understanding of what's beneath the presenting problem. These two things take time to accomplish. Once you have gone through the sequencing above, you will have a better idea of the things your client is willing to do to get things back on track. You need to be clear with them that you will leverage their reputation, resources, and political influence. This is important, because though some clients may have a good talking game, they may lack the dedication needed to follow through on their actions. Once they know that their reputation is at stake, they will either walk away or fully invest in what's on the table. For those of you who are internal full-time employees, this is where you find red flags and future roadblocks. For those of you who are external consultants, this is where you walk away or refer services to another consultant.

TECHNIQUE #2 – RECYCLED PROBLEMS, BAD PERSONALITIES, AND POOR TEAM PERFORMANCE

Let's say a client calls you because they have a team who keeps repeating the same mistakes, which cause delays in delivering to a timeline. This has been happening for a few months and what was occurring with a small group of people is now scaling to a bigger team.

Presenting symptoms include:

- The team complains about a lack of clarity in roles and responsibilities even though they have gone through them several times.
- Teammates are not communicating with each other or engaged during team meetings.
- Teammates are taking things personally and it is dropping their engagement on the project, which leads to anxiety and stress about individual performance.
- The manager is frustrated that the team members are acting like kids and fumbling around.
- The manager has expressed that they don't think people can change.

Figure 3-2 displays what your client typically experiences. They see an event or situation (i.e., trigger), which leads to a perceived series of problems that manifest themselves as collective problematic behaviors. Remember, the average person is highly dependent on the auto-pilot feature we discussed in the mindfulness chapter, so they don't have time to think about what else could possibly be contributing to the presenting problems.

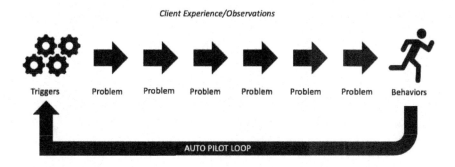

Figure 3-2: The autopilot loop

To help the client identify the patterns that create behavioral problems among the team, we will explore and apply Cognitive Behavioral Therapy (CBT for short)[5] type techniques. CBT helps us to look beneath the surface of problematic situations, identify things that aggregate the problems, and can be used to create new mindsets for people to work with. As a process, CBT reminds us that trigger events rarely act in isolation, so we should always be on the look-out for what lies beneath the surface.

Figure 3-3 shows us that there is a trigger event (e.g., lack of role/responsibility clarity), that leads to a series of thoughts (e.g., someone else should be doing that task or no one told me that's my role, why should I do that?), which then leads people to personalize comments and statements (e.g., who does she think she is, she's always trying to tell me what to do; if he talks about it, he should do it), ultimately leading to a displayed set of problematic behaviors (e.g., missed deadlines, lack of communication, frustration, or poor performance). Going through the cognitive behavioral approach allows you to see and understand that there is much more happening in the space between trigger situations and displayed problematic behaviors.

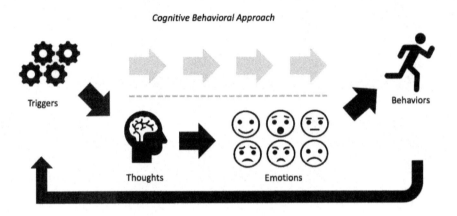

Figure 3-3: Cognitive behavioral approach

Try this: The goal is to help the manager and the team create new ways of behaving. The process of driving new behavior stems from an increased awareness of triggers and thought patterns, which can be achieved by using a goal-oriented approach. I recommend doing the following exercise on a whiteboard with the client alone first, so they understand the process; then, hold another session with the overall team with the manager co-leading the conversation.

Step 1: Start by identifying the behaviors you want to change and the behaviors you want to live-up to. Display these at the individual or team level, it's up to you. It is important to visually display them, so everyone can see the connections and feel the experience.

Step 2: Have the team identify the various possible triggers that they feel create the observed behavioral outcome. The manager is usually a good place to start, as they will be able to call-out the event or situation that usually trigger the undesired behaviors.

Step 3: Be careful here. This part can get emotional and uncomfortable. This is where you get the team to explore how they feel and the thoughts that come to mind when the trigger event occurs. Allow them to express freely without restrictions. It helps to have them write things down on a sticky-note on their own then paste it on the board. Once everyone puts their note on the board, have them work amongst themselves to identify the team patterns.

Step 4: Now you can get the team to focus on the goal-orientation section of the work. By now they have identified triggers, faulty thinking, emotional baggage, problematic mindsets and behaviors. The final step is for them to re-create a workflow using team-based agreements where everyone can agree to support each other. Remind them that behavior change is easy, the difficulty comes with sustaining the desired change and the only way to win is to do it together.

To make sure that the behavior modification sticks, you'll need to apply gentle pressure to the manager by giving them assignments (e.g., constant team check-ins) that have them practice what they are learning (e.g., display role modeling behavior). It will take time for things to stick and for new habits to form, and the amount of time is highly dependent on the manager reinforcing the desired behaviors. The manager is the authoritative figure among the group and is often seen as the parent of the household, so if the "parent" misbehaves or deviates from the intended actions, so will the rest of the family.

TECHNIQUE #3 – MERGING FOR ACTUALIZATION

The foundation of human psychology is that individuals move through the stages of life trying to achieve actualization – a state in which individuals have balance and harmony in the way they see themselves, how others see them, and how they truly are at their core. Whoa, that's a lot of information to process! I feel your pain, so I took the liberty of sketching out a visual I use with clients when we are working on a turnaround plan (either for themselves or their teams). I call this "process merging for actualization", and it was inspired from great psychologists such as: Abraham Maslow[6], Jean Piaget[7], Albert Ellis[8], and Icek Ajzen[9] to name a few.

As we go deeper into this, I want you to be fully aware that "actualization" is temporary, so don't beat yourself up when individuals oscillate out of it. Remember, it is cyclical and people can be trained to sustain it for extended periods of time, but they will oscillate.

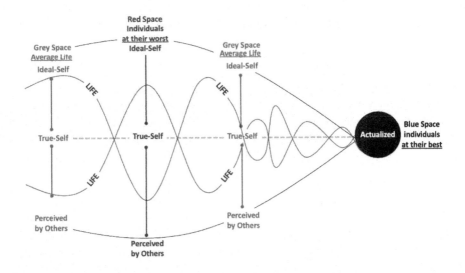

Figure 3-3: Merging for actualization

Figure 3.3 shows three identities: ideal (who we strive to be) at the very top; true (who we really are at the core) the center dotted line; and how we are perceived by others shown at the bottom; the actualized-self is shown as the merging of the three identities within the blue dot. (Note: visit www.theroundtablebook.com or www.thinkdiff-llc.com for images, worksheets, tables, and graphics in color).

Grey Space: this represents the average day for the average person, in which nothing highly memorable or significant happens. This shows up in the workplace as just another ordinary day, mostly because the individual has a proportional balance between the three elements of their identity. Yes, there is a gap between the three, but it's something they are capable of working through emotionally, physically, and psychologically.

Red Space: this represent the phase in which people are at their worst. As you can see, this is the space where the distance between all three identities is the greatest. Individuals who are in this space often bump heads with others, miss deadlines, fail to show-up with confidence or competence, and experience higher levels of stress among many other things. Performance issues arise or get worse because they spend their time trying to merge their identities but fail in the process. The failure feeds a negative mental model, which exacerbates the situation – it becomes a cycle and contaminates others. Sometimes you will hear people express it as, "I had a bad day/week/month/year" or "that person is not a good fit for the culture of this company."

Purple Line: this line represents, LIFE, where we experience highs, lows and everything in between. For simplicity I only draw one line for the client, obviously that line can be shown in many different ways and positions across the continuum of time.

Blue Space: people tend to be at their best and perform at their highest peak when all three of their identities are in balance and have harmony. This means that they are comfortable with who they are (i.e., how they see themselves); others accept them for who they are (i.e., how others see them); and they feel confident and competent in how they show up (i.e., how they truly are showing up day-to-day).

On average, human performance problems stem from a continuous discrepancy between the person's ideal, true, and perceived identity.

The longer these "selves" spend apart from each other the longer people will experience pain, struggle, and bad performance.

Sometimes I joke and say that this discrepancy issue is in our DNA, because the model looks like DNA sequencing when you map it out over an extended period of time.

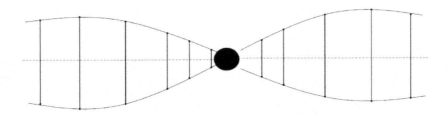

Figure 3-4: The DNA of actualization

Okay, so now that you understand merging for actualization, what can you do about it?

Let's say you are working with a client because they received low scores on their employee engagement survey. The client has been tasked with creating an action plan to get the scores up. For illustrative purposes we will use the following issues: low trust in leadership, lack of perceived professional development, and poor communication amongst the team.

Try this: when working on a turnaround plan with a client, I like to leverage Self Determination Theory[11, 12] to promote motivation and wellbeing in the workplace.

To be specific, I work with the client to create ways to promote their team's sense of autonomy, competence, and relatedness. Here's what the process looks like…

Step 1: Start with a conversation with your client to understand how they promote autonomy, competence, and relatedness within their team. This conversation will give you a soft baseline of the current state. It will also inform you on what you need to do next to shake things up.

Step 2: Remind your client that people will show up their best at work when they feel that they can express their true-selves in the workplace. This is where I walk the client through the visual that I shared with you earlier (Figure 3-4).

Step 3: Work with your client to come up with ways to resolve the target issues. I have worked with consultants who do this through a team workshop or use it as a coaching plan with the client. I find both ways to work, the choice is yours. Table 3-4 is an example of what you can craft with your client.

Target Issues		
Low Trust in Leadership	Professional Development	Poor Communication
⬇	⬇	⬇
Potential Solutions		
Autonomy	**Competence**	**Relatedness**
• Encourage individuals to make key decisions on specific projects. • Provide the team with the freedom to choose various paths of action. • Have the team hold themselves and each other accountable for the plans they put into action.	• Encourage each person to teach others what they know/love doing at work. • Have individuals share the progress of their project and decisions they have made throughout the journey. • Recognize individuals for the work they put into the matter, and for the deliverable. • Invest time, money, and resources into bringing monthly/quarterly trainings that have tangible results.	• Host social events that cater to introverts and extraverts of the group. • Encourage "tag-teams" where a sub-team is created to tackle a task. • Set aside a tea, coffee, smoothie budget where people have a 1:1 with every person on the team to learn about each other.

Table 3-4: Resolving target issues

When you do these things, you will begin to see a notable change with the team. It is mostly because the gap between the three identities comes closer toward actualization. This is the point where people experience happiness, fulfillment, flow, and increased performance. Remember, it is temporary and they will oscillate in/out of this state. Encourage your client to positively reinforce the moments that brings them together, as it will help to extend the periods people experience actualization across time.

Chapter Three

Summary

In this chapter, you learned that as a fixer, you will be involved in projects where people are very emotional, irrational, and may even psychologically revert to a mental state where they are very difficult (or nearly impossible) to work with.

In this line of work, you will get to see the many ways people behave and how they treat each other. The many personalities will show themselves to you as you attend client meetings, listen to arguments, analyze client data (e.g., employee engagement surveys, performance reviews, coaching assessments, etc.).

By now, you realize that for you to be good at what you do (fixing situations), you must be able to help clients who are experiencing stress and change find ways to regain control of their situations.

The techniques in this chapter were designed to help you channel your inner psychologist skills. Not as a therapist, but instead, as a decent, good, kind, and loving person.

☺ Pay attention to your client, you might find what they need ☺

CHAPTER FOUR

THE INVESTIGATOR

"We're all amateur investigators. We scan bookshelves, we ogle trinkets left out in the open, we calculate the cost of furniture and study the photographs on display; sometimes we even check out the medicine cabinet." ~ Lisa Lutz

When I think of an investigator two main professions come to mind: a detective and the employee relations person. If you run a Google search on the job duties of a detective you get something similar to the following… a detective gathers evidence, collects facts about a criminal investigation, interviews possible suspects, witnesses, victims of a crime, and presents evidence to help solve or close a pending case. If you run a similar search on the job duties of an employee relations person you get something to the effect of…provide counsel to staff, provide services to promote workplace wellbeing, protect the rights of the employee, mitigate liability risks for the employer, gather evidence for investigations (e.g., accusations, allegations, policy violations, etc.), interview various parties involved on a case, and keep accurate detailed records of cases among many other duties.

There are many differences between a detective and an employee relations person; however, in my opinion, there is one significant similarity - to investigate. Both professionals do this by keeping clean unbiased records and by reading between the lines of human behavior. Much in the same way that you will be doing with your turnaround plans. If we create a quick job description for your role with clients it will read something like this...this turnaround consultant gathers information to understand the needs of the client; interviews the client to assess the objectives of the future state; interviews colleagues, managers, peers, and friends of the client; provides support to promote progress of the client; and mitigates setback risks among many other duties.

The Investigator Perspective	
Common areas to apply this perspective	• Executive integrations • Process consulting • Team building
Qualities of people in this field	• Interpersonal skills • Problem solvers • Negotiators • Critical thinkers

Table 4-1: The investigator perspective

WHY SHOULD I THINK LIKE AN INVESTIGATOR?

As a turnaround specialist, you need to be prepared for the possibility that clients and various people you work with will at some point withhold information or distort the truth about what's happening with the situation. Chances are that you are not native to the project and trust is something that you will have to earn with the people you are working with. If you are working on a very sticky turnaround plan where someone's job is on the line or you are trying to recover their reputation, you can count on many lies and potholes along the way. This means that you need to be on your best game. Speaking from experience, I know you will not be able to be your best all the time, which means you will need to keep proper records of details and situations to help fill-in the holes.

In this chapter you will read about some basic investigation techniques used by detectives and employee relations staff to run cases, and keep detailed records with the goal of serving and protecting the best interests of their clients. To make things even more interesting for you, there will be times when you have multiple clients within the same engagement (insert suspense music here ☺). An example of multiple clients is when you are called in by a company to help one of their executives get their performance back on track – a last attempt before they are released from the company. In this situation your client is both the executive being coached and the company paying for the service.

THE TRANSFORMATION MODEL

For this particular perspective, you will leverage two components of the transformation model: the reason why your client wants this change, and how you are keeping track of the progress toward the desired outcome. Part of the transformation model is shown below (Figure 4-1) with the relevant section components in bold.

$$T = \sum W \rightarrow \mathbf{?} \rightarrow \mathbf{H^2} \rightarrow (L_T) \rightarrow B \therefore ?$$

Figure 4-1: The transformation model (abridged)

As a refresher:

? stands for "why does your client want this?" Having the truth behind the turnaround plan is important—it will save you a great deal of time and will make your strategy much more efficient. Imagine working with someone to improve their performance, meanwhile the company is planning to terminate them anyway. You are being used as a checklist item for their records. If you know this up front, you can decide to pass on this engagement. Focus on gathering data and facts about the situation.

H^2 stands for "**H**ow will you know you have it (or getting close)?" and "**H**ow are you keeping track?" It is squared because there are two H's in the model. This is meant to remind you to be clear with your objective and measure its progress. For instance, how will you know things are getting better…is the executive you are coaching less of a jerk to their staff? If so, how are you measuring that progress?

TECHNIQUES TO TURN THINGS AROUND

The following techniques that you are about to read are based on typical investigation processes and are presented here to help you think like an investigator. While working on turnaround plans, you will run into situations that require you to investigate, collect facts, analyze data, and decipher the difference between truth and lies. The not so sexy part of this process is that you have to take really good notes– I mean, notes upon notes, upon notes. Yes, a big portion of your time is interviewing people, hosting focus groups, listening to perspectives of various individuals, navigating the details of all the data, history, and background about the case. Don't be discouraged or correlate the investigation process with negative engagements. You will have situations where your services are used to take something good and make it better. An example of this is someone wants to work on ways to improve themselves to get a promotion, or someone needs your help to be more mindful of the promise they made to their family about work-life balance, or you get called to help with something called "organizational integration" – you'll learn about this later. Taking on both types of cases will make you a more balanced practitioner– it will expand your perspective.

TECHNIQUE #1 – PREPARING FOR YOUR CASE

Mental Preparation. Start by getting your mind in-check. It is your duty to be professional, objective, and unbiased. As your engagement with your client evolves, it is your responsibility to keep your relationship from getting personal – it will cloud your perspective. Focus on maintaining a healthy amount of skepticism; it will keep your senses sharp, and increase your ability to decipher the details you need from the garbage you will be fed throughout the process.

Emotional Preparation. As your engagement with your client unfolds and you see progress being made (or not), you need to remind yourself to separate your feelings from your thoughts. It is easy and common for you to "identify" with your client. This is where certain emotions, behaviors, or thoughts are transferred from one person onto another, it typically occurs when we over-step the professional relationship we have with the client. Perhaps they remind you of someone you know, or make you very proud of (or upset over) their progress– it is your duty to separate your feelings from the equation. The moment you let this guard down will also the moment when your perception of patterns– and ability to really help the client– decline.

Preparation Prerequisites. Before you can actually get started helping your client and investigating what it will take to reach the desired objectives, you need an outline of what to do during your investigation. Think of this as the prerequisite phase of the process: a plan of how you will get the information you need to be able to create a turnaround plan for your client. For your convenience, below is a starter checklist. Over the course of time and many clients later, I am certain that you will have a checklist of your own, but for now, this will get you started with a baseline. The process of investigating a situation is explained in technique number two.

ITEMS YOU CAN USE TO CREATE A PREREQUISITE CHECKLIST:

a. Prepare questions for a full in-depth interview with your client(s). During this interview you will gather the following details: who is your client(s), what do they want to achieve, why is this needed or important, when are they targeting its completion, how will they know they have achieved it, and what do they anticipate getting in the way.

b. Have a list of referrals ready in the event that you are asked to handle a situation outside your expertise.

c. Create a list of the people you need to speak with for this engagement.

d. Create checkpoints to remind yourself to remain objective and impartial.

e. Invest in a notepad or computer where you can keep good reliable notes.

TECHNIQUE #2 – WALK ME THROUGH THE PROCESS

Before you take your checklist and run-off talking to people, you need to have an investigation process in place. Without a formulaic process, the questions you ask and path you take may be ineffective. I interviewed detectives and employee relations staff and both said that when you start with a bad process it will lead to an ineffective investigation, which might actually be worse than you not doing the investigation at all. The following steps outlined in table 4-2 are an abridged and modified version of the much longer and intensive process that the people I interviewed follow for their own investigations. These steps should help you begin creating muscle memory of how you approach an investigate process for your client.

Step	The Process	Objective
1	**Project opens**	• Initial client meeting • Initial parameters are outlined for this engagement
2	Interview client(s)	• In-depth client intake about objectives and obstacles • If there are multiple clients you need to have clarity and alignment on the true objective(s) of all parties involved • Get clear examples of what it will look like when the objective is attained • Gather list of people to interview about the objectives
3	Create interview path	• Create a sequence of people you will interview • Determine if you need to host focus groups or other small group sessions • Have list of open-ended and probing questions

4	Provide assessments	• Release the feedback surveys or 360-degree surveys • Some engagements require assessments like MBTI, DISC, or other personality type assessments
5	Interview references	• Conduct interviews in a short timeframe, avoid having long time gaps between sessions • Take detailed objective and unbiased notes
6	Create action plans	• Gather all notes and assessment outcomes • Analyze data, identify patterns, barriers, accelerators • Create (short, medium, long-term) plans based on findings
7	Monitor progress	• Create multiple progress checkpoints • Create intentional micro-corrections to check that your client can recover from minor setbacks, this will build self-efficacy for larger setbacks
8	Create transition plan	• Plan that reinforces behaviors without you being there • Schedule post-engagement checkpoints
9	*Project closes*	• Final client meeting on accomplishments and next steps

Table 4-2: Investigative process

TECHNIQUE #3 – RECORDS: KEEP THEM NEAT, OBJECTIVE, AND DETAILED

You will have many conversations with your client, their peers, friends, managers, people they manage and the like, and I guarantee that you will accumulate a mountain of records. These are just the notes you gather through conversations– it doesn't cover the information you gather through the several assessments you administer. By now, you can see that there are tons of data points and information to sort through, analyze, and keep organized. Take that number and multiply it by the number of clients or engagements you are running and have completed over the course of your time as a practitioner. You get the point; you have a lot of information. I have spoken with many consultants that have found a simple solution to this problem. They simply refuse to take notes; they rely on the information they remember. I am blown away when I hear this. I don't know about you, but there is no way that my brain can hold that much information in a neatly organized manner.

Some of you might wonder…why should I bother with this? Well, here are some reasons why you need to care:

1. Proper notes can help you minimize risk and exposure for you and the client.
2. They can help you to identify patterns of speech or thought (from you or the client).
3. They can be used to refresh your memory on a topic of conversation that you had with the client or person you interviewed.

4. When reading your notes from the third person narrative, you can see opportunities or weaknesses that you might have missed.

5. When your notes are objective, detailed, and accurate, they can be used to resolve disputes between you and the client.

Now that you understand the reasons to capture notes you might be wondering...how do I do it? Great question! There is no right or wrong answer here, but there are good and better answers. I interviewed a bunch of consultants, detectives, and employee relations staff to gather a list of the tools and tips they recommend for capturing good notes.

Note Taking Tools and Applications

- Traditional paper and pencil
- Google Keep
- Microsoft OneNote
- Evernote
- Bear (mobile app)

Note Taking Tips

- Write down who you met with and their role and history with your client.
- Meeting purpose, agenda, or desired objectives.
- Main theme that arises from the conversation (evidence to support, refute, or modify your current understanding of the situation).

- Intended actions for the meeting.
- Practice shorthand, but make it legible.
- Your notes should be as detailed as they need to be. Only you can gauge this one.

Chapter Four

Summary

In this chapter, you learned to spot the holes and inconsistencies in the stories that people tell, but more importantly, you also learned to prepare yourself for the possibility that people will do their best to hide information from you (yes, this includes your very own client).

As a turnaround specialist, you will have cases where you need to investigate, collect facts, analyze data, and decipher the difference between truth from lies. A big portion of your time will also be spent interviewing people, hosting focus groups, and even mediating conflict between individuals - a process that will require you to take many detailed notes.

This chapter provided you with a starter set of basic techniques used by detectives and employee relations staff to run cases, and keep detailed records with the goal of serving and protecting the best interests of the client.

Learning to think like an investigator will expand your perspective, while grooming you to become a more objective and balanced practitioner.

THE RESEARCHER

"Creativity requires input, and that's what research is. You're gathering material with which to build." ~ *Gene Luen Yang*

Next up is for you to refresh your memory on the scientific method. To do so, we will be thinking like a researcher and exploring possible turnaround plans through the lens of research methodology. The role of a researcher requires them to use a scientific approach to get a better understanding of the issue at hand. They do this by experimenting with various scenarios with the goal of uncovering factors that answer their research question. What on earth does the scientific method have to do with my projects and me fixing them? Glad you asked! You see, a turnaround plan is only as useful as the action plan that goes behind it; and that action plan is only as good as the evidence you have that it will work; and that evidence is only as good as the research you have to support your wild-ass guess. I mean your hypothesis. ☺

	The Researcher Perspective	
Common areas to apply this perspective	• Strategic planning • Executive coaching • Culture transformation • Organizational effectiveness	
Qualities of people in this field	• Communication skills • Logical thinkers • Objective "truth" seekers	

Table 5-1: The researcher perspective

WHY SHOULD I THINK LIKE A RESEARCHER?

There comes a time in the life of every fixer when she or he must rely on previous experiences to inform them of the decisions they must make to correct a situation. Ideally, a fixer will rely on healthy evidence-based assumptions when creating turnaround plans. In this role, your task much like that of a researcher is to use a specific set of criteria to make educated guesses/predictions, experiment with scenarios, hold variables constant, keep an eye-out for outliers, and make generalizations from your observed findings about similar future events. See what happened here? A cyclical process at its fullest, all through the scientific method. Don't see it? Don't worry, it will become clearer in the upcoming pages.

THE TRANSFORMATION MODEL

To think like a researcher, we will leverage four components of the transformation model: the objective of your turnaround plan, the reason why your client wants this change, how you are keeping track of the progress toward the desired outcome, and the philosophical question – now what? Part of the transformation model is shown below (Figure 5-1) with the relevant components in bold.

$$T = \sum \mathbf{W} \rightarrow \mathbf{?} \rightarrow \mathbf{H^2} \rightarrow (L_T) \rightarrow B \therefore \mathbf{?}$$

Figure 5-1: The transformation model (abridged)

As a refresher:

W stands for "what do you want?" - since you are likely working on a turnaround plan for a client – the question really is: what does the client want to accomplish?

? stands for "why do you or your client want this?"

H² stands for "**H**ow will you know you have it? and "**H**ow are you keeping track?" It is squared because there are two H's in the model. This comes in handy when making observations and taking notes on the outcomes of things you are testing.

∴ is a logic-based symbol that represents "Therefore" - in the context of how we use it for turnaround plans and the transformation model, it represents a philosophical question

(Now What?). Once your client has reached their goal and you have successfully turned things around, now what? Do you need to rinse and repeat or should you refresh your methodology or approach and (re)execute? The answer to this question will depend on the whole reason you are doing this anyway. If you were called to fix a situation and you fixed it – that's it, you're done. Learn your lessons, pick-up your stuff, move on to the next one. But if the transformation was tied to a long-term goal, you'll need to reflect on this element a bit longer, as it may indicate you have more work to do. Either way, you need to be prepared with a systematic method and process to test your ideas. For that, I encourage you to make friends with the scientific method.

THE SCIENTIFIC METHOD IS YOUR FRIEND

I am running with the assumption that you need a very brief and simple walkthrough of the steps behind this systematic methodology. To refresh your memory, I will simplify this by showing you what it looks like in an ordinary day-to-day life event. Then we'll expand this thinking into a turnaround plan. I like pictures when I read books, so I am using some for mine.

Here we go…

1   <u>Presenting Challenge</u>

Your car won't start – womp, womp!

2   <u>Conduct Research</u>

Has this happened before?
What did you do last time it happened?

3   <u>Generate Hypothesis</u>

Maybe, the battery is dead.

Maybe, fuel tank is empty.

4   <u>Test (Experiment) Your Ideas</u>

 - Inspect power sources.

- Check fuel gauge or leaks.

5   <u>Record Your Observations</u>

6   <u>Make Your Conclusions</u>

Someone forgot to turn off the interior lights the previous night. This drained the battery.

7 <u>Communicate Findings</u>
Now, you can go "yell" I mean remind the rest of your family not to forget to turn off the lights.

Figure 5-2: The scientific method visualized

TECHNIQUES TO TURN THINGS AROUND

TECHNIQUE #1 – THE TESTING APPROACH (A/B METHOD)

Now, that you have the process fresh in your mind, let's explore it as a technique with a turnaround plan. This time we will use a table format (Table 5-2) instead of pictures–I know, I know. Hang in there, you'll be fine.

 Business Challenge: Logistics Center Problems

THE SITUATION:

A newly appointed director of a logistics center calls you because she has noticed that there are a lot of workers who talk about being tired at the end of the shift. The director understands that this is a labor-intensive setting, so she expects some fatigue, but not to the extent of what she overheard being expressed in the breakroom in the recent weeks. Considering that she is new to the role and is concerned about possible workplace dangers caused by fatigue, she calls you to help her turn this around. The following scenario (Table 5-2) is just one of many possibilities to research the presenting problem. As you go through the scenario below, try not to overthink this particular process as there are many ways to approach a solution to the situation.

	Steps	Researcher Notes
1	Presenting problem	• Increased worker fatigue. • Client added staff to alleviate the pressure. • Client is new to the role.
2	Research/investigation	As you investigate the situation you uncover: • The increase in staff during shifts has created other problems: role confusion, idle workers, slowing down work productivity. • Leadership is asking questions about her division's performance given the extra headcount. • Client is concerned her first intervention is making her look bad and is experiencing performance anxiety of her own.
3	Possible ideas	• It's possible there was a recent change in workflow. • It's possible her division has

		assumed more work. • It's possible that work is not efficiently organized.
4	Test your ideas	• You gather evidence to support your suspicion of flow changes. You found new processes have been added to the design. You compare it to the past and they don't appear to be too different from the work done now. You hang on to this clue for the next round. • There is no evidence to show that the volume of work has changed the last 12 months (outside of normal trends). You drop this hypothesis. • You remember a previous engagement where you rearranged workers to increase widget throughput and you think it can work here. You explore this further by creating two groups. The first group will do things like they did in the past (testing your previous clue) and the second group will do things the new way. You have both groups report their level of fatigue at the end of the week. To make things

		more sophisticated, you have both groups wear a small GPS for five business days.
5	See what happens	• The results of the GPS drawings inform you that workers are spending more time walking back-and-forth between tables to complete tasks. This gets you thinking that the recently implemented processes could be what's leading to fatigue. • You and the team rearrange business processes keeping the integrity of the new work and test again. • This time you find increased throughput and decreased fatigue.
6	Make conclusions and communicate findings	• You inform your client of the findings and provide her with recommendations to sustain the observed change.

Table 5-2: Researching potential problem

See how simple and fun that was?!?! Yes, it was simplified for the sake of clarity, so just remember that when you do a full-blown experimental approach it will take much longer, and findings will not jump at you right away. Have patience, keep an open mind, and enjoy the process. Approaching problems with a researcher's perspective takes time and practice. Depending on why you get called in, you will have several options to choose from, and each one of those options will yield different results and generate their own set of problems. Selecting the appropriate research technique is important and it is very common for researchers to use multiple methods to help them arrive at a sound conclusion. Using mixed-methods allows you to control various factors and it also helps you reduce errors that are naturally found in the environment. Here are a few more techniques that you can add to your treasure box of tools.

TECHNIQUE #2 – SURVEYS, ASSESSMENTS, FOCUS GROUPS

The techniques we are talking about in this section will help you keep track of the progress your client is making toward their goal. I like to use them as a combined package, which is why I am grouping them here for you. The most common situation I find myself using these in is when I am serving as a coach. Let's explore what it looks like to use these techniques as a performance coach. Allow me to emphasize that there are many types of coaching engagements, such as, promotions, career transitions, life coaching, skill development, and performance management to name a few. Although each type of engagement has a unique need, in my mind, they all share the fact that your goal as a coach is to help the individual be better than they were before you started working together. There is a great book out there on coaching by the title, *Clueless: Coaching People Who Just Don't Get It.*[15] I like this book because it has a very simple to use approach on the coaching lifecycle; it also includes many insights on various assessments for coaching that you can take advantage of for your turnaround strategies.

Since I like pictures, this is what the process looks like in my mind:

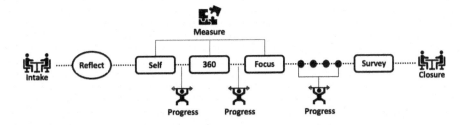

Figure 5-3: Coaching lifecycle

For those of you who prefer a list format, here you go:

Step 1: Conduct your intake meeting with the client.

- What are they looking to accomplish?
- Why is this important for them?
- When do they need to have this "new state" completed?
- Who (or what) will support (or arrest) their development?
- How will they know that they have achieved their goal?
- Ask if they have previously taken coaching or assessment? If so, get access to those assessments and action plans.

Step 2: Take the time to yourself to reflect on their answers. Ask yourself

- Is their goal realistic?
- Are you the right coach for the job? If not, you need to refer this out.

Step 3: Let the baseline begin. The type of tools used depends on the purpose of your engagement. For simplicity, I will refer to them at their highest theme, instead of specifying a type (e.g., MBTI, Hogan, etc.). I like to proceed in the following order:

- Self-assessment to understand their personal views and perceptions.
- 360-degree feedback to get a holistic view from various people.
- Focus groups to dig deeper into the opinions of key people.
- Pulse survey distributed across the engagement. This is meant to gather multiple progress checkpoints.

Step 4: Conduct your closure meeting with the client. The amount of time you work with a client can range from days-to-years. I have found that revitalization projects last anywhere between one month-to-three months. During your final meeting with the client focus on reviewing the progress they have made over time, celebrate their achievements, provide recommendations on next steps, and encourage them to keep the momentum alive.

TECHNIQUE #3 – NATURALISTIC OBSERVATIONS

Naturalistic observation[16] is a method used by researchers to understand naturally occurring behaviors of the subjects of interest. This technique is used when it is impossible to bring subjects into a lab to study them without interrupting the behavior being researched. Think of it this way, the best way to study the reasons why a business culture is toxic is to see the culture in action. This technique is incredibly valuable for us working on revitalization strategies, because it allows us to see and record activities as they are occurring in their natural environment. Observing something in its natural state is straightforward and simple. Instead of giving you a checklist on how to conduct this technique, I will highlight three common scenarios where I find it helpful to use naturalistic observations for revitalization plans: teaming, executive integration, and culture transformations.

OBSERVATION SCENARIO – A: TEAMING

When I define the term "team" I like to use a very rough definition that goes like this: a team is a group of people clumped together to complete a task. Then, I use the term "teaming" to describe a group of individuals who have clear roles and responsibilities, embrace flexibility, collaborate tasks, coordinate efforts/resources, share meaning, and are moving towards accomplishing a shared goal. Don't be fooled into thinking that people on the team have to like each other for teaming performance to occur – you can actually have a high performing team with conflicting personalities. Naturally, a team who likes each other will perform better. From what I have seen, there are few organizations who truly experience teaming performance. I believe that many organizations just have a collection of employees who call themselves a "team." Don't take my word for it– next time you visit a client, take the time to observe the team in their natural environment. All you have to do is watch them. The best way to ensure that they behave naturally is for you to ask your client if you can sit with the team to do your own work. It will take about five-to-nine days before you become just another person in the crowd. It is at this point that people will let their guard down and transition into their autopilot behavior (i.e., natural behavior), this is where you will see them for who they are, at their best and at their worst. If you are interested in seeing teaming in action, I encourage you to watch a basketball, soccer, or football game.[18] If you are not into sports you can also go see an orchestra or attend a concert. You will notice that everyone on that "team" understands who they are, and what they need to do in order to accomplish their mission. For instance, you won't see a flute player want to also play the violin midway through the symphony just to have a "stretch goal." Unlike employees in organizations, who assume they can take on multiple roles within the same project.

OBSERVATION SCENARIO – B: EXECUTIVE INTEGRATION

Executive integration is a plan designed to help new incoming senior leaders to quickly and efficiently onboard to a new organization. These plans are mostly designed for senior leaders since it can cost millions of dollars to hire them and their roles are so unique in the organization, which means they will not have a peer with the same job title there to support them. It is extremely important for these individuals to be accepted by the organization and to understand how to navigate its culture and politics. There are several elements that go into creating integration plans, and many consultants like using 90-day plans. There is a great book out there by the title, *The first 90 days: Critical success strategies for new leaders at all levels.*[17] I like this book because it can be used by anyone and for any level of the organization. The bottom line here is that as you are helping someone integrate, you must invest time and effort into studying the environment they will work in, the people and departments they will oversee, the challenges they must resolve, and current state of the culture they are walking into.

OBSERVATION SCENARIO – C: CULTURE TRANSFORMATIONS

Organizations exist to serve a purpose in the world which they try to accomplish by hiring professionally skilled people who have similar values to those of the organization (e.g., Mission, Vision). The collection of all of these people and their unique personalities make-up what is known as the corporate culture.[19] Over the course of time, organizations will be impacted by various forces (external: market, competitors, politics, societal norms and internal: emotions, personalities, dysfunctions, and leadership views) that will require the organization to adapt to stay relevant and alive in their market. For the average stable organization, culture transformation is not something that should happen very often. In fact, the core elements of the culture should not change. However, there are times when the only option is a transformation. Take for example, mergers or acquisitions (two or more cultures coming together into a larger culture; divestitures (one culture is no longer part of the larger culture, they must find their own identity); scalability growth for start-ups (what once was small and felt like a family is now much larger and new strange people are joining the family); or the most recent craze of digital transformation. In all of these scenarios, a transformation (e.g., turnaround plan) can only begin to occur by observing, recording, and understating the current way of being. A culture transformation is likely one of the most time consuming (often taking years) turnaround plans that you will ever work on. If you are an independent consultant and you land one of these projects, make sure that you are properly staffed to support it and also be very careful that you are not sucked into the culture you are trying to help the client create.

Chapter Five

Summary

In this chapter, you were reminded that the scientific method is your friend. Thinking like a researcher helps you to explore possible turnaround solutions by leveraging research methodology.

In this line of work, we must constantly experiment with new and old ideas. It's often the case that a solution that worked for one client will never work for another client – even though they have very similar circumstances. This means that we must think like a researcher; we must use a scientific approach to get a better understanding of the things we are dealing with in order to be able to formulate a course of action.

As a fixer, your role much like that of a researcher is to use assessments, surveys, focus groups, naturalistic observations, and hands-on experiments to be able to make educated predictions on behalf of your client.

Just keep in mind that there are multiple ways to arrive at a solution. Yes, selecting an appropriate research technique is important, but it is even more important to keep an open mind about the problem – don't be afraid of using multiple methods to help you arrive at a solid conclusion.

MIDWAY TOUCHPOINT

Up to this point, you have learned about mindfulness practices, and to take care of yourself first before helping others. You have gained a deeper appreciation of paying attention to the needs of your client in the way a psychologist would. You have a richer understanding that establishing a clear path to investigating your client's needs; coupled with taking detailed, objective, and unbiased notes, will significantly increase your chances of success while reducing risk when working on a turnaround plan. After reading the last chapter, you are now more cognizant of the importance of leveraging research and the scientific method to test your solutions.

In the following chapters you will learn about specific qualities of a diagnostician, air traffic controller, campaign strategist, and lawyer that you can use to help you create impactful turnaround plans for your clients. Before digging into the next chapter, I want to take this time to remind you of the round table visualization we used at the start of the second part of this book. The items in bold within the image below (Figure 5-4) represent the personas and lessons that you have unlocked thus far. The grayed-out items will be unlocked in the following chapters. When a challenge presents itself before you, just remind yourself to visualize these professionals sitting with you and utilize the skills they bring to the round table.

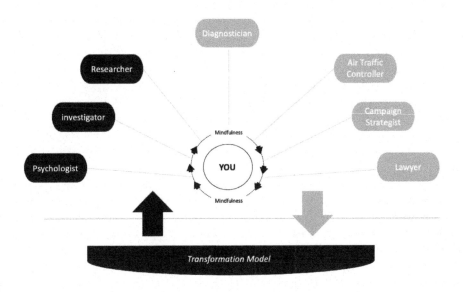

Figure 5-4: The round table

CHAPTER SIX

THE DIAGNOSTICIAN

"Bedside manners are no substitute for the right diagnosis." ~ Alfred P. Sloan

In very simple terms a diagnosis is a summary given to describe a collection of problems or symptoms along with its potential causes and treatments. For those of you interested in a lengthier much more sophisticated definition, I encourage you to venture over to what Webster says in the medical section of their online dictionary.[21] A diagnosis can't exist without a trained professional to bring it to the surface. For that you have a diagnostician: a professionally trained individual who specializes in making different types of diagnoses. These individuals have deep and wide knowledge of their industry, which allows them to have acuity for the various clues that collectively explain the presenting symptoms. A diagnostician can be found within the medical profession (as a type of medical doctor), the education system (as a special needs learning consultant), or the mental health industry (as a psychiatrist).

Guess who else has skillsets like a diagnostician? That's right...you do! Much like a diagnostician, your goal is to evaluate the presenting symptoms of your client from every possible angle, in order for you to get as much of the picture as you can. The solutions you generate are highly dependent on internal and external forces– sometimes generating a solution will be as easy as creating a training plan and other times it will be as difficult as creating an entire culture transformation.

The Diagnostician Perspective	
Common areas to apply this perspective	• Organizational resistance • Retrenchment strategy • Customer or employee experience (e.g., journey design) • Productivity performance
Qualities of people in this field	• Interpersonal skills • Critical thinkers • Ability to solve complex problems • Ability to see connections (e.g., see the whole picture)

Table 6-1: The diagnostician perspective

WHY SHOULD I THINK LIKE A DIAGNOSTICIAN?

Continuous learning is important for diagnosticians because they must be aware of historical cases, current research, and patterns that may indicate changes in the near future. One can argue that this is important for every professional, which is why I highly encourage you to think like a diagnostician. Thinking like one means that you must keep up with trends; understand the landscape of tools and assessments within your reach; stay connected to the community within your industry; find creative solutions; integrate findings and implications from other industries or case studies into your action plans. To say it another way, thinking like a diagnostician will help you to see the entire picture and better prepare you to create thoughtful, innovative, comprehensive, and holistic turnaround plans.

THE TRANSFORMATION MODEL

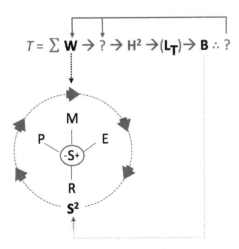

Figure 6-1: The transformation model

As a refresher:

W stands for "what does your client want to accomplish?"

LT stands for "how much time do you have to work with?"

B stands for "Barriers or Blockers" that <u>**will**</u> get in your way. Be vigilant! There will be things that will get in the way of turning things around. The quicker you identify what they are, the faster you can create mitigation points. I encourage you to keep your eye on people (emotions, behaviors, patterns) and processes (ways of doing things or not doing them), as these will be related to challenges you are dealt with.

Physical - **M**ental – **E**motional relate to levers you need to pull and apply a negative, neutral, or positive **S**timulus to obtain a desired outcome (**R**esponse).

S^2 stands for "Support System." When you begin turning the situation around, you need a reinforcement system to keep it all together. The last thing you want is for it to fall apart once you roll-off the project.

TECHNIQUES TO TURN THINGS AROUND

The following techniques and models were created using foundational elements of medical, educational, and psychological diagnostic approaches. I created the models shown here for business turnaround practices; you will find that they follow a similar systematic approach to "diagnosing" a situation such as those used to diagnose an ailment. The approaches that work for me are shown in the images that follow; feel free to take these models and adapt them to your own profession, industry, sector, or segment. The bottom line is for you to do what's best for you and your client.

Let's dive in.

TECHNIQUE #1 – DIFFERENTIAL DIAGNOSIS ("THE TURNAROUND DIFFERENTIAL")

This technique is found within the medical profession and it used as a process to examine a presenting set of symptoms that look alike or share very similar components, which makes it difficult to diagnose as one thing or another. According to Wikipedia[22] and Webster's dictionary,[23] going through a differential process allows practitioners to gather evidence from various points of view with the aim of explaining possible causes and identifying factors that help them see subtle differences, which then enable practitioners to make informed decisions about potential treatments. The structure of this process is simple and elegant: you start with the main symptom(s), then you run through all possible logical known scenarios of what could cause it, what it could be related to, and what could be used to treat it. I use a similar structure for turnaround plans–mine has some fun sprinkled into the process because I use various colored sticky notes. I call it "The Turnaround Differential" and it looks like this...

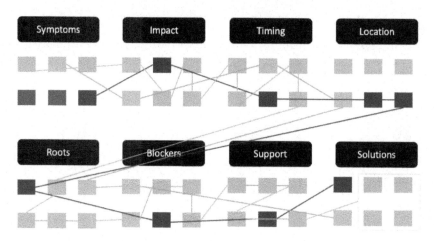

Figure 6-2: The turnaround differential process

(Note: visit www.theroundtablebook.com or www.thinkdiff-llc.com for images, worksheets, tables, and graphics in color).

Use the space below to sketch a differential of your own.

Here's a legend to explain each item and its use:

Box Name	Each Sticky Note
Symptoms	Different symptoms, behaviors, challenges
Impact	Impact on the organization, team, self, or individuals
Timing	When do symptoms, behaviors, or challenges come to the surface
Location	Places it occurs (is it widespread or isolated)
Roots	Possible causes and triggers
Blockers/Barriers	What is getting in the way (or could) of it stopping or getting better
Support System	People or things available to support, promote, and sustain progress
Solutions	Possible solutions based on patterns

Table 6-2: The turnaround differential legend

Figure 6-2 shows various color sticky notes, each one of them is meant to represent something unique. While going through the process, I find it helpful to use a string to map similarities–this helps me to uncover patterns or trends. This technique can be done in a physical format, meaning you use an office or conference room, pick a wall and start drafting. Alternatively, this can also be done in a digital format, using a laptop and software. An extra tip for this technique is to do it with other people in the room. Perhaps, you are co-consulting on a project or there is a team assigned to it that you can work with. The more ideas you can generate to differentiate true problems, possible root causes, and potential solutions the better off you will be in getting this project back on track.

TECHNIQUE #2 – STREAMLINED THREE STEP APPROACH

This technique is something you can use when your client gives you very little time to work with. The need for this type of technique tends to arise when someone is being transitioned out of one team and integrated into another team or department. A worst-case scenario is that you will get asked to coach someone (on a short time-frame) with deep performance issues which others have failed to uncover the root causes of, leaving it up to you to figure it out and solve it.

The steps are as follows:

> **Step 1:** Collect all the information you can about the issue. This includes all possible historical artifacts, like past assessments, previous client engagements with outcomes, engagement scores (when dealing with teaming interventions), organizational charts and reporting structures, and informal/ formal reviews or complaints. During this step, you are only collecting information that is readily available; you are not generating any new information of your own. You just need to consume, analyze, and interpret available data.

Step 2: Generate a running list of possible causes. This time you are only focusing on one thing and you are taking your client's word that the problem is truly the problem.

Step 3: Once you have possible causes identified, you can create a list of recommended solutions. Since you won't have much time to make proper corrections, you'll need to create a priority list for your client. I have seen some consultants use a sizing effort approach (small, medium, large), in which each recommendation is linked to a level of effort and expected return of investment. I'll save you the suspense– it's likely your client will decide to go with small effort with small gains. After you and the client agree on the recommendation you can implement the action plan. That's it you're done. Move on.

TECHNIQUE #3 – ESTABLISH A STRONG SUPPORT SYSTEM

After going through the differential and uncovering potential reasons why your client is struggling to keep up their performance, you can move into action planning and establish a support system to increase the likelihood that the behavior will stick. Refer to the (Figure 6-3) to remind yourself what it looks like when we link it back to the transformation model. The "**B**" represents barriers/blockers getting in the way, which can be reduced by creating a system that reinforces positive behavior and reduces less desired behavior, shown in the image as **P**hysical - **M**ental – **E**motional levers with the application of a negative, neutral, or positive **S**timulus to obtain a desired outcome (**R**esponse).

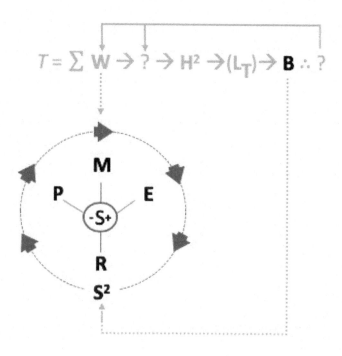

Figure 6-3: The transformation model

This part of the model was inspired by B.F. Skinner's work detailed in the book *Science and Human Behavior*,[24] in which he argues that human behavior can be predicted and modified. Do you remember the saying – *"you can lead a horse to water, but you can't make them drink"*? Well, B. F. Skinner had an opinion on this - there is an excerpt in the book (Skinner, 1965; pg. 32) where he is talking about an experiment in which he is manipulating specific variables to induce his subjects to drink water. According to Skinner, not only can you bring a horse to water, but if you control the right circumstances, you can also get the horse to drink. Of course, he said it much more eloquently:

"It is decidedly not true that a horse may be led to water but cannot be made to drink. By arranging a history of severe deprivation, we could be "absolutely sure" that drinking would occur... If we are to predict whether or not our subject will drink, we must know as much as possible about these variables. If we are to induce him to drink, we must be able to manipulate them... we must investigate the effect of each variable quantitatively with the methods and techniques of a laboratory science."

~ B. F. Skinner ~

I am not encouraging you to deprive your client of drinking water, but I am saying that much like Skinner increased the likelihood of his subjects drinking water, you too can increase the chances that your client's new behaviors will stick. To do that, you must understand all of the historical variables that influence the behavior your client is interested in improving. The concept I use goes something like this: to change the current behavior, I have to change the future behavior by modifying its history today. Oh, wow, that's mind-twister. Don't worry, I created a visual to help you understand what I am talking about with this concept.

Figure 6-4 represents my interpretation of what we see through our day-to-day interactions. As you can see, it starts with something triggering the behavior we observe (or are guilty of projecting to the world ourselves), which concludes with the impact it has on our friends, family, and colleagues.

Sometimes, these actions and the outcomes of these behaviors can be a tough pill to swallow (hence, the shape of the image – get it ☺).

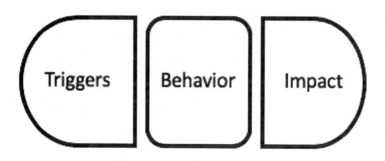

Figure 6-4: Triggers, behaviors, impact

Visualize something with me…

Imagine that you are in a lab setting inspecting possible scenarios that will lead you to a diagnosis, and in this lab, you have a microscope. Now, imagine looking into that microscope: as you adjust the zoom a little, you begin to see new things happening that were not so obvious to you before (Figure 6-5). For instance, you are now able to see that behavioral triggers (arrow #1) dip into historical events, which in turn, create reinforcing variables (arrow #2) that encourage and strengthen the behaviors that are displayed to the world (arrow #3).

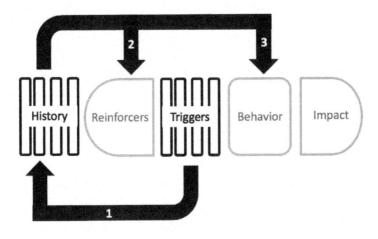

Figure 6-5: The triggers, behaviors, impact loop

With that same imagination, I want you to once more adjust the magnification to get a little closer to the details. Aha! Now, you can see behavioral patterns! This is the point at which you need to create behavioral pattern disruptions and generate ideas of the types of support that your client will need to sustain their desired behavioral change over time. The ideas will come to you through the different iterations you go through with the client. Researchers suggest that behavioral disruption to create new behaviors is most benefited when the person trying to change sets intentions about the future and how they see themselves behaving in it.[25] To say it another way, the magic happens when you and the client work to intentionally create "new history." The process is straightforward. Refer to figure 6-6, specifically, the 2nd movement – pattern disruption. Here is where you assess the given scenario, test possible solutions or interventions, and evaluate their impact and effectiveness. If the previously tested solutions don't work you will need to cycle through the movement again, until you find the best application for your client's needs. The moment you find something that yields a viable outcome, you should quickly integrate that into the client's daily habits. This sets you up nicely for the third movement of your process, which is to establish a support system with the client.

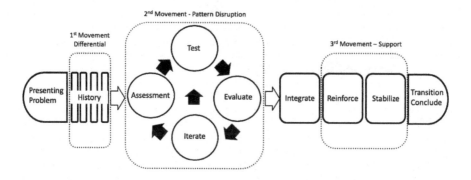

Figure 6-6: The triggers, behaviors, impact movements

Remember, the average person is using behavioral patterns that they have built over time and placed on autopilot. It takes a great amount of effort for people to be actively mindful of every move and decision they make throughout the day; therefore, creating a pattern disruption is key. Getting someone to change their behavior is easy: all it takes is self-awareness and a little sprinkle of effort on their part. However, sustaining the new behavior long enough for it to become a new autopilot habit can be very difficult to accomplish.[26] For that you will need to bring in reinforcements and an entire support system to go with it.

Think of the support system as a person or group of people who are equally invested in the success of the turnaround plan. For this part of the movement, you need to take advantage of the fact that humans process and perceive the world around them through their senses. I have found that working directly with physical, mental, and emotional conditions promote greater sustained behavioral transformation.

Let me show you what this looks like in practical terms.

Let's say that you are working with a client who has behavioral issues–more specifically, your client is seen as combative and unappreciative of their staff. To speed up this example, we can fast-forward to where you and the client are aware of the problem and the client is willing and motivated to "try to change." What would you do…tell them to be nice? Figure 6-7 depicts what it looks like when you use a support system to help your client create progressive transformation. I imagine B.F. Skinner saying something like - we need to support the horse in its quest to drink water. I'm not saying your client is a horse or looks like one…

This time around, I want you to visualize the support system components of the transformation model shown in (Figure 6-3). Use the microscope from your previous visualization. Go ahead and adjust the magnification a little more. Got it? Here's what you will see (Figure 6-7). Interesting, right!?! Not to worry, I am going to break it down for you and walk you through what this means for you and your client.

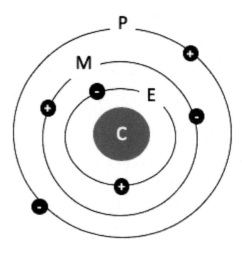

Figure 6-7: The client atomic structure

The client is at the center of the support system (represented by everything surrounding the middle- C). The positive and negative bubbles represent reinforcers and detractors, which are people who will work with you and the client. The support system needs to have both of types of people, because one will focus on promoting and encouraging positive behaviors, while the detractors are tasked with constructively challenging the client to ensure that the client practices what they are learning. Having your client practice will help to further solidify their newly acquired behaviors. Think of it this way, you and the client need to identify various people within their immediate network of family, friends, and colleagues who are willing to participate in the support system and play a specific role (e.g., reinforcer or detractor). Once those individuals are placed and everyone knows their roles, you can now move into the (physical, mental, emotional) elements of the model. The best way to explain these elements is through the use of a table (Table 6-3).

Element	Examples
Physical	• Rearrange the physical environment to conduce desired behaviors. • Provide client with tools that make things easier to perform. • Leverage technology to create reminders or action items toward the goal.
Mental	• Provide the client with mental scripts they can use to coach themselves throughout the day. • Expose the client to meditation or mindfulness practices/techniques. • Co-create visualization schemas with the client, which are useful during times of stress or pressure from detractors. • Encourage the client to invest in self-learning practices, perhaps watch short video clips or read relevant material on the topic of focus.
Emotional	• During your coaching sessions you can have them practice the following elements: o Active listening o Participative communication • Have reinforcers in the support system provide the client with verbal encouragement.

Table 6-3: The client atomic structure legend

ON YOUR OWN

When we opened this chapter, I mentioned that diagnosticians are found within medical, educational, and mental health professions. For those of you interested in a deeper understanding and appreciation of the diagnosis processes, I encourage you to pick up two books: the first is for medical knowledge by the title, *Improving Diagnosis in Health Care,*[27] the second book is for mental health knowledge by the title, *The Diagnostic and Statistical Manual of Mental Disorders.*[28] These books are wonderful resources covering the diagnostic process. When you read through them, keep in mind that these are designed and meant for use by licensed trained professionals with years of experience and special skillsets that allow them to decipher, interpret, and apply into practice. The takeaway message is for you to understand and appreciate the systematic approach those fields must follow, so that you can apply a similar data driven systematic structure in your own profession and for the needs of your client.

Chapter Six
Summary

In this chapter, you learned that clients will come to you with a variety of presenting symptoms. They will give you a lengthy list of pain points with varying degrees of pain. There will be times when your client believes that they already know the solution to their problems, they just need you to execute it for them.

In most cases, you will find that their presenting symptoms (or perceived solutions) are rarely the actual problem (or way to fix the problem– this means that clients are simply describing a collection of problems). Your job (and where you add value as a consultant) is to help relieve their pain. To do that, you must understand all the places it "hurts", and then find the potential causes and treatments to their pain.

This chapter provided you with techniques to think like a diagnostician. By thinking like a diagnostician, you are able to evaluate the presenting symptoms of your client from different angles, so that you can get a more holistic picture of the issue at hand. You will find that the solutions you generate will depend on internal and external forces, which means that you must keep up with trends; understand the landscape of tools and assessments within your industry; stay connected to the community within your field; find creative solutions; integrate findings and implications from other industries into your turnaround plans.

Thinking like a diagnostician will help you to see the entire picture and better prepare you to create thoughtful, innovative, comprehensive, and holistic plans to revitalize a failing situation.

THE AIR TRAFFIC CONTROLLER

"The big ones make the little ones shake" ~ *Anonymous Pilot*

The profession of an Air Traffic Controller (ATC for short) is not one that gets much publicity or hype by the general public. Why? My guess is that it is simply overlooked and not seen as something interesting by many people–maybe they don't think that being an ATC is as cool as being a pilot. Not me, I have much appreciation and respect for the work they do and the stress they deal with on a daily basis. To help give you some perspective this is how Study.com (an online education provider)[29] describes the duties of the Air Traffic Controller profession:

"Air traffic controllers regulate air traffic either within an airport's airspace or air traffic between airports. They communicate weather changes, visibility issues, wind conditions and nearby aircraft to pilots, using radar, computers or visuals to monitor aircraft in the assigned airspace. Air traffic controllers may give landing and departure authorization and instructions. They may also determine and direct flight path changes as necessary."

For those of you who already knew that - you are probably wondering what it has to do with turnaround strategies. Hang in there, I will get to it. First, let's review what you can expect to cover in this chapter. We will start with a brief overview of what a day in the life of an ATC looks like and what they do up in those towers (spoiler alert, some of them are not in a tower. What?!? Yeah, I know). This sets up a nice foundation for us to make a transition into how thinking like an ATC can help you with your turnaround strategies (Table 7-1). We finish the chapter with techniques designed to help you keep things in flight.

The Air Traffic Controller Perspective	
Common areas to apply this perspective	• Digital disruptions • Technology implementations • Project management • Leadership development (i.e., management interventions)
Qualities of people in this field	• Communication skills • Task and resource management • Collaborators • Risk mitigators

Table 7-1: The air traffic controller perspective

Table 7-2 depicts a very simplified and generalized description of what a day in the life of an Air Traffic Controller (ATC) looks like. Keep in mind, that the role of an ATC will vary by position and the airport/airspace that they are responsible for looking after. With that in mind, the given description is not meant to be specific to a location or role, rather, it is designed as a sample summary.

Okay, here we go. A day in the life...

Time	Task
4:00 – 5:50	Wake-up, get ready for work, commute to work (ATC is a 24hr environment, so an ATC can have different shifts – this describes an average morning shift).
6:00 – 7:00	Get briefed on relevant events from previous shift(s), obtain briefings on current weather conditions and any other procedural duties for current shift.
7:00 – 8:30	Start first position (ATC's rotate between 3 or 4 positions, which include: approach, en route, tower, and ground control).
9:00 – 9:30	Break – these are extremely important (more on this later).
9:30 - 11:00	Second position (ATC's work each position a minimum of 40 minutes to a maximum of 90 minutes).

11:00 – 11:30	Lunch
11:30 – 12:00	On the job training. It is critical for all ATC's to study and be familiar with all things found in the FAA Order 7110.65 - this is a procedural and regulation handbook that they must live and operate their daily lives by (often referred to as the "ATC Bible").
12:00 – 13:30	Third position.
13:30 – 14:00	Break
14:00 – 15:30	Fourth and final position for the day.

Table 7-2: A day in the life

There you have it. A simplified version day in the life of an Air Traffic Controller. Obviously, the timing and tasks will vary depending on needs, but what is important for you to understand is that ATC's have a tightly packed schedule with very little room for error. It is also worth noting that ATC's share a responsibility of caring for the lives of hundreds of thousands (millions for heavy traffic airports) of people traveling to and from their airport/airspace.

WHY SHOULD I THINK LIKE AN AIR TRAFFIC CONTROLLER?

Over the course of your career, you too will share the responsibility of caring for the wellbeing of many individuals. Here's how I see the

ATC work translating into our line of work and the transformation model. People like you and me help the client regulate the flow of their emotions when situations are difficult; we must keep the channels of communication constantly flowing as things can change by the minute on any given project; we must make use of technology and any surrounding resources (e.g., support systems) to help us make informed decisions and to monitor the progress of the changes we implement. Lastly, we provide clients direction and reinforcements to proceed given a desired path or course of action.

THE TRANSFORMATION MODEL: SUPPORT SYSTEM ELEMENTS

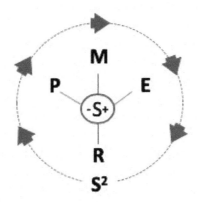

Figure 7-1: The transformation model: support system

To help you think like an Air Traffic Controller we will start by covering a few key insights. These insights were attained from researching ATC's who work in a highly stressful, highly regulated, and highly communication dependent environment. The cool part is that these insights are transferable to the turnaround strategies you get to work on.

INSIGHT #1 – BE CLEAR, INTENTIONAL, AND CONCISE

Air Traffic Controllers and pilots don't have the luxury of engaging in an ordinary sentence-based conversation. In fact, the aviation community has a specific set of phrases to help them keep communication between key personnel clear, intentional, and concise. The entire purpose of their method is to convey and to express only the necessary information to complete a task. Take the following excerpt as an example of communication (stripped of any fluff and unnecessary details). It is something that a pilot might use to make the initial contact with a tower or a facility specialist...

"New York Radio, Mooney Three One One Echo."

Easy, right? Just for fun, the excerpt below is my interpretation of what a fluffy unnecessarily lengthy one-way aviation conversation looks like. You won't find a pilot or ATC engaging in this type of communication, especially, if it is a heavy traffic airport/airspace location.

* * *

"Hey there New York radio tower, how are you? I hope that all is well on your side. I'm doing good. Anyway, I just want to call you because I want to let you know that I am actually on my way now to arrive there at your location. Umm, I hope traffic there is light, not like that last time, ugh, such a pain. This time I am in a different airplane, so keep a look out for me in the – umm- hold on, oh yeah, in the Mooney with my plates reading as three hundred eleven with an 'e' for echo at the end. See you soon."

* * *

As you can see, the first example is much cleaner and easier to understand compared to my lengthy fluffy paragraph.

Don't worry, I am not asking you to learn a new language or to speak to your clients using aviation phrases. Here's what this means for your turnaround strategies and communication flow between you and your client. Focus on establishing clear communication channels as it will allow everyone involved to understand their assigned duties, which will enable each person to execute with minimal distractions and to the best of their abilities.

Many of you have likely encountered a client who likes to "think out loud" – I don't know about you but keeping up with their free-flowing associations and deciphering what is needed versus what is "extra information" can be very draining and time consuming. Trust me, it takes time and effort to train your client on using ATC style communication, but it is well worth the effort. Just start by being a role model of what you want the communication to look and sound like; make it crisp and intentional.

Taking this insight from ATC's is useful for those of us working on turnaround strategies for two reasons. First, by keeping communication simple between you and the people involved in your project(s) you will be able to focus on the important stuff – you know the things that actually matter to moving the progress needle. Second, this style of communication will allow you to have a clear understanding of what you are working on with your client and why it is important to them. These reasons become increasingly important as you work with higher level profile clients. The upside of high-level clients is that they understand and appreciate clean and clear-cut communication. Heck! Sometimes I have to ask for them to tell me more, especially, when they provide one-word answers. There needs to be a balance between communication that is too short and communication that is far too long.

For those of you interested in learning more about radio communication within the aviation community, I encourage you to pick up a copy of the Federal Aviation Regulations/Aeronautical Information Manual (FAR/AIM) and take a look at the Radio Communications Phraseology and Techniques section of the manual.[30, 31] Happy reading!

INSIGHT #2 – ALWAYS BE LEARNING

This insight is simple, brief, and to the point.

There are many things outside of the control of an ATC. For instance, weather, mechanical failures, or route alterations by other locations. Although, they can't directly control these things, they are able to mitigate potential risks and work through the problems presented. To do that they must be quick thinkers and problem solvers. It takes time, practice, and tons of learning for them to perform at the levels required by the FAA. In order for them to achieve that level of experience they must always be learning. ATC's learn something new at every point of their shift. For example, when they start, they are briefed on current location events and weather. During shifts they might encounter a new situation or new piece of equipment that requires them to "get-smart" on. They are also required to participate in on the job training covering various topics, including changes or modifications made to their "ATC Bible" by the FAA.[32] At the end of the day, some may even study weather patterns and forecast, so that they can transition assigned duties to the next ATC taking over their position or shift.

So, what does this look like for a turnaround strategist like you?

Think of it this way, as you start a project or new client engagement you will get a briefing on the current situation, perhaps also have some historical information on the case. Then as you advance with the project and encounter situations you have never encountered before; you pick up learning material to get smart on the topic at hand. Some of you have special licenses or certifications that require education credits, so I encourage you to expand your insights and learn something new – don't be like some consultants who just get credit for the sake of getting credit. To cap this off, the best kind of learning you will get is found on the job, working directly with the client—knowledge gained by doing stretches your thinking and challenges your mental models–at the end of the day, making you a smarter professional.

Taking this insight into the turnaround practices will make you much more valuable to your clients. By staying on top of the current strategies or innovations crafted by others in the field, you will always have ways of being able to help your many clients. Don't allow yourself to settle into following a single path or one methodology. There are so many of them out there–take advantage and always be learning. You can take it a step further by taking what you learn and finding ways of teaching others – pay it forward. It is our duty to make things better whenever and wherever we can.

INSIGHT #3 – THE BIG ONES MAKE THE LITTLE ONES SHAKE

One of the many things that ATC's get to see every single day is when airplanes takeoff and land – it's part of the job. In much the same way, you too get to see projects that are launched (some even have big parties to initiate the kick-off) and you also get to see projects that come to a "successful" closure. For you as a fixer, you get an added bonus: you get called for engagements where it appears that all of a sudden, the project comes to a complete stop or worse, the players within the project begin to behave irrationally. Your task is to turn this situation around and get it back on track.

In my mind, this is the equivalent of what the aviation community refers to as – wake turbulence – which is turbulence produced by a heavy, slow, and clean configuration airplane. As noted in Skybrary.com (an aviation safety education website), this type of turbulence generates vortices that come off the wingtips and creates a dangerous downdraft of wind for surrounding airplanes. The result can be catastrophic for nearby airplanes–it is worse for smaller airplanes because they have a slim opportunity to recover, especially if they are flying through it during takeoff or landing.

Let's translate how this applies to turnaround work. You see, projects will ordinarily go sideways or stall because of bigger projects (or personalities) entering the smaller project's pathway. Take for example, a company is working on team interventions to generate increases in employee engagement scores (you are not part of this project), when suddenly the company decides to shift directions and calls you in to help them with a reduction in workforce plan plus an organizational design.

In this scenario, the bigger project and its wake turbulence cause the smaller project to halt. I once had a pilot instructor say to me "watch out for wake turbulence caused by these big boys, the big heavy airplanes make the little ones shake." This always stuck with me and has become an eye-opener when working with clients. I often ask the client if there is another project or something else bigger preventing the [stalled] project and its team members from taking off or getting back on course. It seems like eight out of ten times the answer is yes, but for some reason the client doesn't see a relationship or the need for me to be aware of those details.

Now that you have a few key insights to help you think like an Air Traffic Controller, we can transition into techniques to help you with your turnaround strategies. The following techniques also link-up to the support system elements of the transformation model.

TECHNIQUE # 1 – BUILD AND LEVERAGE A TEAM TO DRIVE PERFORMANCE

In the aviation community there is something by the name of CRM and it stands for Crew Resource Management. The concept originally came to existence as a methodology to minimize [pilot] errors. The idea is to minimize distractions and maximize the use of all available resources to increase safety. According to the FAR/AIM part 121, the purpose of a CRM is for...

"...the effective use of all available resources available to crewmembers, including each other, to achieve safe and efficient flight."

This makes sense, everyone (pilots, cabin crew, ground crew, ATC's, etc.,) shares responsibility in the care of lives, so they focus on leveraging all possible resources to make safety and efficiency a priority. After the creation and implementation of CRM, safety increased and errors decreased. A few years after CRM matured, a similar program was created for ATC's by the name Air Traffic Teamwork Enhancement (ATTE for short). As the name suggests, this program is heavily focused on teamwork and communication between and among controllers, and has shown to yield similar positive effects as the CRM.[32]

There is an interesting simulation study conducted by researchers at the FAA, in which they had participants simulate tasks and then view playback recordings of themselves or the team in action.[33] The logic is that by watching playback footage of performance (individual vs team) the ATC's will see where they can improve and put the corrections into action. The natural thought for most of us is that if you focus on you and your actions, the rest of the elements will fall into place. The researchers found that focusing on teamwork performance builds cohesion and task coordination, which leads to overall increased performance of ATC's.[33] The interesting part is where the researchers argue that effectiveness increased as a result of individual teammates having to spend less time trying to solve interpersonal problems.

You're probably thinking, yes, the less they spend on social problems the harder they can work on their tasks, which leads to greater performance. Well, you are on the right track, but the researchers argue that it is actually the shared mental model of teamwork that is the actual culprit of increased performance. Without a doubt, each member must be good at their given tasks, but it is the focus on improving teamwork and communication that actually drives performance among ATC's.[33]

Unfortunately, you won't have ATC's on your team, but you can build equivalents. As you approach the next situation with or for a client and it calls for you to think like an ATC, I want you to mentally visualize a CRM or an ATTE type of team. There is no way that you will be able to get this "airplane" (i.e., project) back on track without the help of a co-pilot and crew. So, I want you to think about all of the available resources you have on hand (or those that you will need), and make sure that you take advantage of their skills and put them to work. All of you are in it together and all of you share the responsibility to help the client achieve their goals.

Sometimes, you will not have anyone of value on the client's site, so you will need to bring in your own resources. Some of you may have a practice with available staff, others will need to tap into your networks to get the job done. On a personal note, I like to keep a consultant bench and skills inventory handy. I know that I will not have all of the answers and solutions for every single client, which means, that I must be able to quickly partner with someone who has the skills or experience that I do not have. You can create your own consultant bench using a template like this one in table 7-3.

Contact	Company	Rates	Services Offered				
			Coaching	Succession Planning	Employee Relations	Employee Engagement	Diversity
Name 1	Company 1	- Hourly	X		X		X
Name 2	Company 2	- Daily				X	
Name 3	Company 3	- Project		X			
Name 4	Company 4	- Retainer	X		X		X

Table 7-3: The consultant bench

I also recommend creating a bench for each client you work with or project you get pulled into. I want to point out that the list of services offered or the employee skills listed on these tables are not exhaustive. In fact, you should modify them to fit your own particular needs. Some of the templates I have are twenty-five columns wide – your templates don't need to be that way or follow my format. The bottom line is that you need to have something you can use for your CRM or ATTE type of team. [33]

Table 7-4 illustrates a sample for what your bench could look like within the client site or dedicated project team.

Name	Department, Team, Role	Notes	Employee Skills				
			Storyteller	Influencer	Trainer	Instructional Designer	Excel Guru
Name	Receptionist	Liked by many people and well connected	X	X			
Name	Marketing	Expressed interest in getting involved with HR projects	X			X	
Name	HR	Friendly, but has a bad reputation with specific business groups			X		X
Name	Manager	New to the company		X	X		

Table 7-4: The client talent bench

As you are building out the team (or network of consultants), I encourage you to build cohesion and collaboration based on a shared mental model (i.e., shared purpose, goal, or mission). Remember, you will fail if you try to revitalize the situation by yourself, so establishing a common team goal and direction will help you get things back on track and move towards the desired performance in a much quicker timeframe.

TECHNIQUE #2 – TASK MANAGEMENT: TIME IS MONEY

Speaking of time - the longer a project is idle the more money it costs you and your client. I am certain that neither you are interested in throwing away money. However, there are some peculiar special occasions where some clients are willing to spend more money to save a dying project instead of letting it fizzle out. I'll spare you the suspense—emotions and reputations have something to do with those types of engagements. All this is to say that ATC's, project managers, and you share a goal and accountability of keeping things moving, on-time, with success, and with money on your mind. In simple terms, the better every one of these roles is at managing their duties and responsibilities, the more money saved (and in some occasions the more money made). The following scenarios describe how task management impacts time and how time impacts money.

The ATC's tasks and the monetary impact.

> For you to get a visual appreciation of what I am about to describe, I encourage you to find a small local teaching airport. Ask the pilot school if they will let you sit at the observation

bench near the taxiways. This bench is typically used by pilot instructors who are watching their students fly solo. If you want to make things more interesting, you can download an app (https://www.liveatc.net) and listen to the local ATC radio communication.[34] As you sit there, you will see how ATC's prioritize traffic management. You will see and perhaps even hear the pressure ATC's experience. More importantly, you will notice the difference across various levels of ATC experience. You will notice how they manage flow of airplanes trying to get onto the taxiway, how they manage pressure from pilots rushing to be called first in line for takeoff. You will notice the additional pressure from those entering the landing pattern and their wishes to be among the first to land and get off the taxiway.

Wonder why ATC's are rushed and where some of the pressures are coming from?

If we hold safety reasons constant, everything else is related to time and money. The smaller private airports are typically used by privately owned small aircraft pilots, private jets owned or chartered by celebrities and business people, and lastly schools teaching students to become pilots. According to Investopedia (an educational website on wealth management)[35] a small single engine airplane (typically used by pilot schools) can have a starting cost of approximately $200 per hour (this number will vary upwards depending on the type of aircraft). Note, this starting cost is only the use of the airplane– it doesn't factor in the cost of the instructor and other fees. Now, imagine the cost for a jet – these can range in the thousands per hour. Therefore, the longer an airplane sits idle the more money it costs. So, you can count on ATC's being pressured to effectively manage traffic flow. Time is money!

Let's translate this into client work and the things you can focus on to maximize monetary impact.

We trust that most project managers have the best intentions to keep things moving, leveraging the resources available to them, and keeping the running costs of the project down as much as possible. However, we also know that they are only one person trying to balance the needs and shifting priorities of dozens of moving pieces, including the demands of the executive sponsor. I argue that having multiple project manager positions will increase the success and flow of the initiative. A person can be assigned to handle resource management, another can be assigned to handle costs, and another can be assigned to manage meetings and logistics. This is my equivalent of the various ATC positions we talked about earlier (i.e., tower, ground control, etc.,). However, chances of an executive sponsor assigning more than one project manager to an initiative is very slim. As a result, you get multiple roadblocks and hiccups that could have been prevented through efficient [traffic] task management. Throughout client engagements, I have noticed that the average project stalls (or completely derails) because there is a misalignment of scope; team and individual goals are not integrated into measured performance;

there is poor collaboration and cohesion amongst team members; or people are acting in isolation running their own agendas which often conflict with the overall project.

So, what can you do about it?

As I mentioned earlier, the best and most efficient thing to do is to breakdown the role of a project manager into multiple key roles. Since that is not likely an option for you, the next best thing is for you to help the project manager. No, I am not saying you need to assume the role of a project manager, instead, I encourage you to have laser-like focus on a handful of key activities that can help you turn the situation around. By targeting the activities in table 7-5, you will be able to maximize the very little time you have to get the project back on track.

Leave these activities to the project manager	Invest your time on these activities
Defining scope	Scope alignment and execution
Activity planning	Leadership and management involvement
Sequencing of activities	Risk identification and mitigation
Resource acquisition and management	Resource cloning and scalability
Scheduling or Work Breakdown Schedules	Monitoring progress

Budgeting and cost estimates	Course corrections
Vendor management	
Within team communication	
Project quality control	

Table 7-5: Focus of time

TECHNIQUE #3 - CHECKLISTS AND DASHBOARDS

The proper and frequent use of checklists and dashboards will help you to drive consistent and efficient performance. Even better, after you run a few projects and are exposed to various client engagements you will have enough historical data to help you to prepare for (and to some extent, anticipate) future screw-ups.

Let's start with checklists. I see them as a way to inform you of what you need to do and what you should be keeping track of throughout different phases of the project.

In the aviation community checklists are used all the time, regardless of the person's years of experience. Don't fall into the misconception that checklists are for amateurs or people who can't keep it together. Checklists exist for a reason. To be more specific, in aviation, checklists are designed and used to help people follow operating procedures and for them to know what to do in case of an emergency. For example, ATC's have a series of checklists and mnemonics that they use when unusual or emergency situations present themselves. According to Skybrary.com (an aviation education website), some common situations include but are not limited to: bird strikes, mechanical failures (brakes or landing gear), bomb threats, problems with communication equipment, power/electrical problems, engine failure, fires, in-flight medical emergencies, and so on. As you can see, this is only a short list of potential situations. You can be sure that the list of possible situations is much longer. This should also inform you that it is not practical (perhaps even impossible) for a single person to memorize every single step for every single situation, especially, if it is a rare or unusual occurrence. Therefore, having a checklist becomes incredibly important.

As you relate this to client work, checklists can be used across the entire sequence of your engagement. For instance, you can have a checklist before you agree to the terms of a contract: to identify problems; to select interventions or coaching assessments; or to transition, exit, or conclude your engagement. In the beginning you will be inclined to have a very long list of items on your checklist, and this is understandable--you want to make sure that you are not forgetting anything. A word of advice, though: don't over think it, just focus on the bare minimum operating procedures. Approaching the process this way will allow you to get a checklist going. As you advance, you will have plenty of time to make adjustments from the lessons that you learn along the way.

Let's run through a basic situation together to get you thinking about the approach you can take to create your own checklist.

The situation...

An administrative director of a local hospital calls you because they are experiencing a pattern of declining performance. The administrator has identified a dip in performance that runs across the last three quarters. They are classifying the problems as a decrease in revenue, drop in staff performance, increase in error rates, lower reported employee engagement, and a decline in patient experience scores. The administrator oversees the business operations department, and her team of internal consultants hasn't been able to figure out how to proceed, so she asks you to jump in and help.

*Note, the purpose of this exercise is not to solve the situation. All I want you to do, is to think about the type of checklist (and items) that you need in order for you to be able to jump in and help your client turn this situation around.

This is a sample plan checklist (Table 7-6). I don't typically share my checklist with clients, it is just a way for me to make sure I am keeping track of key tasks or milestones. Use this as a starting base and modify it to fit your project needs.

Sample – Project Checklist	
Before you start the work	
You understand the client need	☐
Your specific scope for this project is clear to all parties involved	☐
You have relevant material to help you dive deeper into the situation • What has changed to create observed problems (external and internal forces) • Revenue historical patterns • Data on staff performance • Data on employee engagement • Data on patient experience • Tracking, progress, monitoring method(s) • Operating manuals, procedural handbooks	☐
As you start (and do) the work	
The target end-state (i.e., outcome) is clearly described and understood by all resources	☐
All relevant people that will work with you on this project are identified	☐
Clear roles and responsibilities between all key project resources are established	☐
You have a Work Breakdown Schedule/Structure (WBS)	☐
Communication strategy and methods are created (or at least outlined) • Between you and the client • Between project leads and sponsors • Between sponsors and the stakeholders	☐

• Between sponsors and the community at large	
Mandatory and optional meetings are created and scheduled	☐
Barriers and challenges identified (e.g., risks identified)	☐

Design and develop relevant task execution material
   • Staff performance plan
   • Employee engagement plan
   • Patient experience plan
   • Training strategy and plan
   • Revise operating procedures or manuals
   • Update training content (as necessary)
   • Monitor and maintain communication tactics
	☐

Implement and monitor task execution material
   • Training outcomes
   • Final operating procedures or manuals
	☐

Progress checks with client (1:1 meetings)	☐
Closing project work	
Review observed project outcomes with client	☐
Train and transition key tasks to specific resources on the project	☐
Notify appropriate stakeholders of transition and what they can expect	☐
Collect final billings and other administrative duties with client	☐

Table 7-6: Sample project checklist

In the preceding section we covered the use of checklists to keep you informed of actions that you need to take. In this next section, we will cover dashboards and how you can use them to monitor progress and make decisions to get situations back on track.

Okay, let's talk dashboards.

The moment an aircraft takes-off and begins climbing altitude it is being monitored and tracked by someone across different locations. ATC's stay with the aircraft (they transition from one ATC to the next) the entire time (from pre-departure all the way to post-landing). ATC's and pilots each have a dashboard of their own that they use to monitor progress and keep track of key performance indicators. Next time you board an airplane, take a look at the cockpit and you will see the dashboard the pilots are working with for the duration of the flight. Heck, you don't have to wait that long. Just go out to your car, sit in the driver's seat, turn on the ignition and look right in front of you – all of those pretty lights and glowing indicators – yep, that's your dashboard. It provides you with key information that you need at the moment you need it. If you are running low on gas – there is an indicator for that. If your tire pressure is off – there is an indicator for that. Forgot to close the trunk – yep, there is an indicator for that.

I am sure you get the point. I encourage you to think about your projects in the same way. In other words, ask yourself: how can I create a dashboard that is meaningful for me and for my client? The operative word here is "meaningful" – don't go crazy and create an overly complicated dashboard, just stick to the basics and keep it simple. If the project is running low on fuel (i.e., people are burning out) you need an indicator for that. If you implement a change to get things back on track – yep, you need an indicator for that. Effective and clever use of dashboards will help you in many different ways, especially when you are showcasing a set of metrics to demonstrate to your stakeholders that your turnaround strategies are actually working as intended.

How can a dashboard help me turn things around?

> To be clear, the dashboard itself is not a tactic or technique to get a situation back on track. Instead, a dashboard is merely a tool that will help you to visually see progress, trends, patterns and the like. It is through these indicators that you will be able to make informed decisions and, in some situations, take risks. Keep in mind, the dashboard is only as good as the data that's being entered, so, the common phrase "garbage in, garbage out" applies here.

What types of situations can or should I use a dashboard?

> A dashboard can be used for practically anything your heart desires. Of course, this is assuming that you have the data for it. My advice is to be very selective and keep it simple. To get you started, table 7-7 highlights a couple of corporate turnaround situations and the typical components you can include in your dashboard. For a full range and collection of dashboards, I point you to the internet. Type in "corporate dashboards" and you will

have way more options compared to what I can show you here in this book.

Turnaround Situation	Dashboard Components
Employee turnover	• Work schedules • Engagement scores • Pay curves and equity distributions • Team cohesiveness and collaboration reports • Recognition data • Corporate culture • Career mobility

Crisis (public relations)	• Public opinion before the event
	• Public opinion at the moment
	• Media presence across platforms
	   ○ Internal (how employees feel)
	   ○ External (social media handles)
	• Tactic implementations
	   ○ Roadshows
	   ○ Press releases
	   ○ Commercials

Decision recovery	• What was the decision • Reasons for the decision • Decision downstream and upstream impact • Financial impact • Corporate culture impact • Public impact

Table 7-7: Key dashboard components

How do I create a dashboard?

If you are comfortable with spreadsheets and formulas you can create a custom dashboard using all of the data points that you are interested in. You can design the look and feel according to your tastes and needs for the project. If you decide to go this route, it can be a bit more time consuming, but the final product is to your desired specifications. I recommend taking a weekend to create a few different templates that you anticipate needing for future engagements. Don't worry about making them perfect or having all possible elements, just get the basics. The rest will come to you when you start your next client engagement. An even better ideas is to outsource this task, get a professional to help you. The idea is for you to have something created ahead of time, to save time when you actually need to use them.

Some of you are probably saying…" that's great, but what if I don't have the technical experience or the time to sit there all-day creating dashboards from scratch?" For those of you who fall into this category, I recommend purchasing software or pre-made templates.

Are you curious about which one to purchase?

It all depends on what you need, but a quick internet search will provide you with tons of information and options of companies willing to sell you something. There are companies who will sell you a bundle of Excel templates, others will sell you a subscription to use their proprietary platform, and others will sell you a service. Obviously, the price will vary significantly with the option you decide to go with. Just, use your best judgement for your need, don't buy the luxury platform if all you really need is a template. Sometimes, your client might have a platform that you can leverage for their project, all you have to do is tweak the elements. Better yet, the client likely has an Excel guru that can help create a dashboard for the needs of the project. Whatever you do and whichever option you go with, keep it simple – don't let the process of running and maintaining it become a time sucker. You have much more important things to do for your client and the success of the project.

SOMETHING TO CONSIDER: TAKE BREAKS

I want to close this chapter with one last insight. Take breaks!

To be a successful ATC you must have mental sharpness, be able to quickly and efficiently oscillate between high levels of stress to low levels of stress, and adapt to a diverse set of workflow tasks. Sounds familiar? Yep, you too must be good at these things.

The difference between ATC's and you, is that they are required to take breaks. In fact, they can't work a single position more than 90 minutes. The thought is that by giving them a break from the high degree of mental focus they must engage in (especially, during high traffic volume) they will be much more efficient at their job. You on the other hand, are likely working long hours - days, weeks, or months at a time.

Guess what?

Living that lifestyle will take its toll on you and the quality of your work. Trying to do it all, all the time, for everyone will eventually burn you out. Burnout is not good for business. Even the World Health Organization considers it to be problematic, as of May 28, 2019, burnout is now considered "occupational phenomenon" defined as…

- Feelings of energy depletion or exhaustion;
- Increased mental distance from one's job, or feelings of negativism or cynicism related to one's job; and
- Reduce professional efficacy.

Remember: only you know when it is time to rest and recover. Only you know when you have taken on too much. Only you know when you need to refer out clients to your partners or network of consultants. Only you know when to pull the cord. Taking care of yourself will keep you fresh to generate high efficiency thinking.

Chapter Seven

Summary

In this chapter, you learned the value of thinking like an Air Traffic Controller (ATC). You learned that continuously evolving your education is important. You don't want to be the rusty outdated consultant using methodology from years ago. Stay current. Stay relevant. Stay ahead.

By thinking like an ATC, you are now more aware that not all projects are equal in value. This means that when a bigger (more important) project comes along, it will definitely and without a doubt stop or push around all of the other smaller surrounding projects.

In this line of work, we rarely have the luxury of time, which means that having an efficient team is critical. Efficiency is created and nourished by having super clear and concise team roles and responsibilities. While working on a turnaround plan, spend time on having everyone involved be clear on what they should be doing, when they should be doing it, and why they must be doing it.

You also learned time is an important commodity, especially, when there is little of it to work with. This mindset teaches you to keep communication simple between you and the people involved in the plan. Doing this enables everyone to keep focus on the important stuff.

Seeing failing projects through the lens of an ATC also helps you to see that one of the best ways to show your value to the client is by leveraging implementation checklists and dashboards. Never spend your time on a project or effort that you cannot measure through a performance indicator – it will be a waste of your time, because it will be impossible for you to show the ROI to your client.

Lastly, you are only as useful as the creative and strategic advice you can provide to your clients. If you are tired or burned-out, you might as well excuse yourself from the engagement. There is no glory or victory in working an insane schedule – your ROI to the client should be based on the value you provide, not the number of hours you work. Only you can control this, so remind yourself to pause and to take breaks.

CHAPTER EIGHT

THE CAMPAIGN STRATEGIST

"If you're not controversial, you'll never break through the din of all the commentary." ~ Roger Stone

How do you take an issue that people don't care about and make it into a hot topic of discussion or debate? Think like a strategist. How do you take a "nobody" and make them into a "somebody?" Think like a strategist. How do you take a crisis and convert it into "hope" or desire for "change?" That's right! You got it! Think like a strategist.

The Campaign Strategist Perspective	
Common areas to apply this perspective	• Crisis neutralization • Establishing a brand or identity • Situation (re)evaluations • Strategy positioning • Mergers, acquisitions, spin-offs
Qualities of people in this field	• Create brand momentum • Get people to rally around a theme, topic, or issue • Connected to the community and key players in the industry • Resilient • Visionary

Table 8-1: The campaign strategist perspective

This chapter provides you with a handful of techniques used by campaign strategists, political consultants, media manipulators, and corporate advisors to create something out of nothing, lead corporate turnarounds, and stabilize a crisis. When it is all said and done, you will be better informed in ways to help your clients take a failing project, revitalize it, and get things back on track.

To be clear, I am not advising you to favor one political view over another. Nor am I pushing any political agendas of any kind.

Whatever your political point of view is – that is entirely your choice. I am simply providing you with insights used by strategists and other media manipulators, regardless of who or what they represent. The takeaway for people like you and me is to take advantage of techniques that work. How you decide to use the insights and techniques is also your choice.

Let's kick this off with two interesting quotes related to politics and campaign strategy. The first is attributed to Richard Nixon in a 1994, New York Times publication (by Roger Stone, a political advisor), in which Nixon was asked to attend the Republican National Convention to give a speech (to praise Bush or bash Clinton). The full article archive can be found on the NYT website.[38] Within that article there is a particular section that I find very interesting; the quote reads as follows…

"…the only thing worse in politics than being wrong is being boring."

The reason I ask you to pay attention to this quote is because the underlying meaning and message speaks volumes about the things some people are willing to do to stay relevant and in the limelight. The word "politics" in the quote can be modified and replaced with practically any other word and have the same powerful impact. For illustrative purposes, go ahead and replace it with the word "business" or "being a celebrity" or "artist" or "being a friend" – of course, some of these are dramatic examples, but you get the point. It is this type of thinking that gives birth to two communication paths: one used to drive positivity, hope, and optimism, and the other used to drive slander, negativity, and harsh criticism. Both paths create a desire for people receiving the message to move and to act in favor of or against something.

This leads me to the second quote that I want to bring to your attention.

The second quote comes from Ryan Holiday, the author of a book titled - *Trust me, I'm lying. Confessions of a media manipulator.*[39] In this quote, Ryan is describing how he uses (negative) human emotion to drive action and momentum to spread a message across the masses. It reads as follows...

"Things must be negative but not too negative. Hopelessness, despair – these drive us to do nothing. Pity, empathy – those drive us to do something, like get up from our computers to act. But anger, fear, excitement, or laughter – these drive us to spread. They drive us to do something that makes us feel as if we are doing something..."

~ Ryan Holiday ~

This way of thinking is powerful – you see the first quote is basically focusing on the persona of an individual or an entity. However, the second quote, is taking advantage of an existing message and putting a wrapper around it (e.g., anger, fear, excitement, laughter) before releasing it to the world. As you read through the rest of this chapter you will understand how thinking like a campaign strategist and using very simple communication tactics can help you and your client to turn around a situation that is falling apart.

WHY SHOULD I THINK LIKE A CAMPAIGN STRATEGIST?

There is a moment when individuals and companies find themselves in need of a campaign strategist. The need can be a result of something positive (like, starting a new business) or something negative (like, a company having to react to a bad public relations issue). Unlike politicians, not very many individuals or companies actually know that they need a campaign strategist, even worse, they don't actually know these people exist outside the world of politics and if they do, they don't realize that they can use them. Often, I have seen companies (responding to bad press) use a marketing person or legal write something up. There's nothing wrong in having legal respond to bad publicity, but the impact is different when the message is informed by a campaign strategist.

You might be asking yourself, why the heck would I need to think like a campaign strategist or political advisor if the client I am working with is a small barbershop who is looking to expand their business?

Simple, your barbershop client is likely expanding into a new neighborhood, where the market is different from the original shop. They will need new staff, and they will absolutely need new customers. To accomplish those goals, the barbershop needs people to be aware of their new location, they need more followers and supporters – all of which can be attained by having a crafty campaign strategy – hence, the need for you to think like a campaign strategist.

Much like running a corporate turnaround strategy, a campaign strategy leverages a specific series of steps to drive action and participation from the surrounding community. The techniques positioned throughout this chapter are designed to help you mentally embody the persona of a campaign strategist as you create your very own strategy – one in which you create something out of nothing; one in which you have a community of people involved in the greater good.

THE TRANSFORMATION MODEL

As you think like a campaign strategist and begin to craft a strategy of your own, you will be focusing on a few key elements of the transformation model. You will target elements outlined below in bold (Figure 8-1).

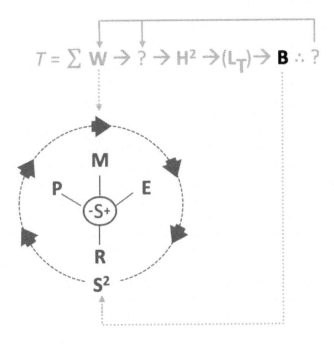

$$T = \sum W \rightarrow ? \rightarrow H^2 \rightarrow (L_T) \rightarrow B \therefore ?$$

Figure 8-1: The transformation model

W – have a clear and super crisp focus on what your client wants to accomplish and why they are asking for help on this matter.

LT – know how long the presenting problem has been an issue and what was done in the past to improve it or make it worse. You also want to know how much time you have to work with to help them turn things around or to respond to a crisis.

B stands for "Barriers or Blockers" that **_will_** get in your way. You may need to run polls, surveys, or focus group in order to fully understand and appreciate the emotions, behaviors, and processes related to challenges you and the client are dealt with.

Physical - **M**ental – **E**motional relate to levers you need to pull throughout the lifecycle of the campaign. All of which will be carried and supported by the community (i.e., S^2 - "Support System") you gather to rally around the presenting challenge.

The following bullet points highlight a few situations in which it would benefit you to think like a campaign strategist.

Presenting problem: A new sales system is being implemented across an organization. The technical team is quickly building components and pushing widgets into a production environment. However, the actual users of the system were never included in the configuration or development conversations of the system. In other words, the sales organization is getting something thrown at them with which they have had no prior involvement.

How you can help: To help the client in this situation, you can create a mission driven campaign. You need a reason for employees being impacted to feel like they are important, like they matter, and that they have a "say" in what happens to them throughout their work day. People can overlook you not including them in the beginning, but they will make decisions about the future and their involvement (i.e., resist or advocate) from the way you make them feel through the process.

Presenting problem: A small CPA firm is going to change their pricing model (i.e., increasing the rates on existing customers) and also plans to simultaneously release a new product they want all customers to use moving forward.

> **How you can help:** A brand awareness campaign is useful in this situation. Changing prices is common and expected (within reason), however, changing a product or service can often be difficult to deal with – people like what they like, and they partnered with the client in the beginning because of what they originally offered. The focus of this campaign is to create a perceived need and value add for the new product or service. In other words, help customers to see why and how the world will be better for them as a result of this new direction.

Presenting problem: A healthcare system is experiencing pressure from continuous turnover of key staff. At the same time the talent acquisition team has noticed an uptick in the number of revolving door candidates – these are people who leave the company and come back to the company in a different role. The healthcare system identified that the number one reason why staff separates, is because they feel that there is no room for growth or opportunities for internal mobility. This explains the revolving door. The problem is that a series of internal mobility programs were created a year ago. It seems that the programs have very little awareness rates, as there are a very low number of employees who are taking advantage of the programs available to them.

How you can help: To help the client in this situation you can put into play an awareness and favorability campaign. The campaign should be composed of an endorsement committee (i.e., leaders doing roadshows to promote the programs), an advocate group (i.e., staff who have directly benefited from the programs), and a street team (i.e., people who wear t-shirts, distribute goodies, and bring awareness to the programs).

There you have it – the above bullet points are just some very brief and simple examples of how thinking like a campaign strategist can help you help your client. Next up...techniques!

TECHNIQUE #1 – BUILD A CAMPAIGN STRATEGY

There are numerous ways to create a winning campaign – the ultimate goal is to win! There is a great quote on this topic in a book titled - *Campaigns & Elections: Rules, Reality, Strategy, Choice*[40] – which reads as follows...

"A campaign strategy is a proposed pathway to victory, driven by the understanding of who will vote for the candidate and why they will do so. "

I love this quote because it calls out the major critical focus points of any strategy: a pathway to victory; who; and why. In my opinion, these three ingredients make up the spirit of an entire strategy. Having said that, this section highlights some of the major must-have elements of a campaign strategy. The beauty of these elements, is that they are transferable and applicable for you and your client's objective.

For you to have an easier time grasping these concepts and to understand how you can begin using a campaign strategy right away, I am including table 8-2 for you to see how I use campaign terms in an interchangeable manner with transformational project-based work.

Political Terms	Consulting Terms
Candidate	Executive sponsor of the project (sometimes it will be the actual product)
Running mate	Co-sponsor(s) of the project
Running message	The purpose of the project, initiative, objective
Backers, sponsors, financial supporters	Finance team or key stakeholders
Political committee	Executive committee
Political director or scheduler	Project manager
Volunteers	Street team
Coalitions	Change agents or advocates of the project

Media outlets	Communication channels
Voter base (i.e., database)	Impacted community
Research (supporters, opposition)	Impact assessment, adoption studies, progress metrics

Table 8-2: The interchangeable campaign terms

Next, we will use an example of a false start (i.e., failed launch) technology implementation project to explain how a campaign strategy can be used to turn a situation around.

Presenting case: A furniture manufacturing company ("the client") calls you in to help them create an internal communications campaign. They tell you that they are getting ready to kick-off the start of a new technology implementation project and they want your help. The client informs you that they are on a six-month timeline to get this out to their employees. At face value, there are no red flags and it all it sounds very simple. You take the client on and begin to join meetings with the rest of the intact team. One month into the project you notice that something is not adding up: during discovery conversations with people outside of the implementation team, you get the sense that people are resisting the project (even before it is launched). You decide to probe deeper into this and ultimately find out that this project had failed previously and created a big negative ripple effect across the organization. To make matters worse, the client refuses to change the name of the project and has decided to move the six-month timeline into a four-month timeline.

Summary of case:

- The timeline is now four months instead of the original six months.
- The client refuses to change the name of the project (which has a bad reputation to start with).
- The employees are aware of the previous failed project and have a negative perception towards it.
- No one on the implementation team knows how to create or execute a communicating plan.

Campaign Strategy Elements: you can quickly put together a campaign strategy for "Initiative X" using the elements in figure 8-2. These elements are inspired from *The Political Campaign Desk Reference*[41] book a guide used to help political professionals create winning strategies.

Campaign Strategy Main Elements

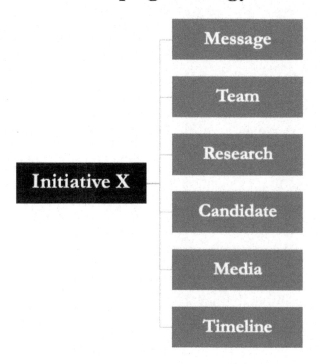

Figure 8-2: The campaign strategy elements

Action Plan: Let's dive deeper into crafting the action plan using the campaign strategy elements.

> **Message** – you need to be very clear, crisp, and concise on the message that you want to create for "Initiative X." Remember, you want your message to be exciting and to drive action based on feelings generated from the campaign. It can be tricky to get this down and it might actually take you a few different messages to get the one that speaks to your target audience. If you had more time to work with, you could craft a message by

talking to the people. To do that, you would need to hit the streets (so to speak) and talk to those being impacted by "Initiative X." After talking to about a dozen employees across different segments, geographies, or departments you would then able to create a message that resonates with the community. A message that would stick and expand (i.e., becomes viral within the organization).

However, in this case you don't have time on your side. To speed things up during a tight campaign timeline you can target making changes to a few basic human conditions in the workplace. The items listed below are not an exhaustive list, but they have worked for me in the past. They include crafting a message around:

- Job security (e.g., removing, adding, or modifying roles).
- Role design (e.g., making work easier, modifying job related tasks and activities).
- Financial impact (e.g., rewards or degradations).
- Physical environment designs (e.g., going from cubicles to open spaces, change of seats).
- Psychological safety (e.g., perceived pain, pleasure, challenges to group thinking, trust).

By tapping into these conditions, you will certainly hit triggers that spark action. Remember, you are dealing with a failed launch, so you first need to publicly accept the fact that it failed before the community can move past it and join you on a new direction.

Perhaps, you can create a corny, funny infomercial talking about the initial attempt to launch. Do not spend too much time talking about it or apologizing for it – just acknowledge it and move on to your new campaign strategy message.

For illustrative purposes, we will target sales teams within the manufacturing company, using the following message…

"Initiative X, a new system for a brighter future"

The message is simple, easy to remember, and vague enough to indicate positive changes are happening.

Next, you can focus on having the right team in place to help you spread the message.

Team – in order for a campaign to be recognized by a broader community, the right mix of people needs to be brought together to make things work. The majority of the time you will be walking into pre-existing teams – a collection of people put together by a project executive sponsor. If you are lucky, you will have the right people to start with, and all you will have to do is to make sure that they all know their proper roles and responsibilities. But, hey, if it was easy, they wouldn't be calling you.

In this part of the campaign strategy, you first need to focus on getting the "right" people on the team and second, you need to make sure that they are clear on what you need them to do.

The Dream Team

Executive Sponsor: The role of this team member is for them to be the face of the entire project. They should have full commitment to the recovery and success of this project. It is extremely common for these players to say they are in it for the long run, but many of them simply make a single appearance and quickly disappear. Then, they get upset when the project goes sideways. Think of the executive sponsor as the candidate running for office – they are found everywhere and have deep knowledge about the campaign (i.e., project). I like to get a one-on-one meeting with this person the moment I roll onto the recovery project. Here, I set the foundation and make it clear that the entire campaign is based on them and they need to be prepared to put things on the line, like: their reputation, resources (materials and people), financial investments, and time.

Co-Sponsor: This role supports the executive sponsor brand the campaign to the public.

Think of them as the candidate's running mate. They are there for the long-haul and share the same responsibilities and commitments as the executive sponsor. Both roles are be used to spread the campaign message.

Financial Backer: This is the person in charge of holding the project financial backing. This is the second person I meet with during the initial phases of my involvement. I recommend for you to get acquainted with them (as soon as possible) as they will tell you how much money can be allocated to the campaign. Chances are that they will give you a very small (or zero) budget, that's fine – just remind them that the last time they took that approach they had a failed launch. So, if they want to repeat the pattern, they can use the same formula and do it without you. For those of you who are launching a product by a third party (like a software or technology provider) you can easily get that provider to sponsor your campaign. Just be aware that they are not doing it because they are kind people; they are doing it because they want something in return. When a third party backs your campaign, they have a vested interest and at some point, they will call you to do something for them. I recommend keeping everything within your control, and minimize third party involvement as much as possible. I would even challenge you to avoid it if you can, for as long as you can.

Project Managers: I recommend having a project manager to handle the timeline/logistical events and another project manager to take care of conversations and task management between and among teams. You are guaranteed to get pushback on having multiple project managers, but do your best to get the additional support. Sometimes you can bring in an aspiring employee who is trying to build their portfolio for their next promotion, or perhaps you can use an intern (this route will be more time consuming and you have to be mindful of not violating any internship laws). Worst case scenario, you can fill in the gaps on the strategy work. For this, refer to the Air Traffic Controller chapter, specifically the task management section.

Campaign Manager: Think of this person as a hybrid between a marketing agent and a change management practitioner. They need to be versed in design, as well as the psychological principles behind humans moving through the experience of change. This person will need to get people to experience the Kübler-Ross five stages of grief[51] in a very short period of time.

Street Team (Experiential Team): This is going to be a group of people—ideally, one that embodies a diverse representative sample of your target audience. This is the team that will be tasked with creating hype and movement around your message. They will wear shirts with the message, they will take photos with people across the organization, they will create experiences and interact with your intended audience.

For ideas on how to use an experiential (street) team, I ask that you venture off to YouTube and search for the following videos:

> Example #1 – Search for: Coca-Cola: Happiness starts with a smile.[42]
> Example #2 – Search for: Zappos – Pay with a cupcake.[43]
> Example #3 – Search for: Examples of Experiential Marketing – Disha Kanchan.[44]

The sole purpose and goal of your experiential (street) team should be to make employees feel happy when they are around. The happier employees feel when your experiential (street) team is around (while wearing clothing with your message), the more they will attribute positivity with the things your project is trying to accomplish. The negative feelings of a failed project will quickly diminish and convert into positive momentum based on the things your experiential (street) team is doing.

Change Agents: This team is also referred to as an advocate or champion of change. Although the names are different, the concept is the same. Think of them as a group of subject matter experts selected and embedded within different teams and departments across the organization. They are put in place to help their peers feel emotionally and psychologically supported throughout the process of change. These are the people the general community will rely on when things get bad (and they will). Make sure these agents have the support they need to actively and rapidly respond to matters as they arise.

Influencers: Every organization has a set of corporate influencers. They are the equivalent of celebrities within a corporate culture. These are the employees who are deeply connected, trusted, and respected throughout the organization. Be very mindful and strategic when you use these corporate influencers. Yes, their voice is very powerful, but it is also very easily diluted if you use them for every project or for every message.

Endorsers: The moment you begin to build positive momentum (and I mean immediately after something positive shows up) you should activate the use of endorsers. These are impacted stakeholders who were once against your message and are now in support of your project goals. They are the community of employees who have directly received something positive by being involved with "Initiative X."

Okay, now you have the dream team in place. Next-up, is having a clear understanding of your community base. In other words, it's time to do some research on the employees being impacted by "Initiative X."

Research – In order for you to be able to convert bad perceptions into positive awareness, you will need to get to know your community base. In a typical political campaign this is done by pollsters, analyzing previous campaign research data, conducting door-to-door research, purchasing voter historical data, and so forth. Considering that "Initiative X" does not have much of a runway, priority of work is key for you in this situation. You will still need to conduct some level of research, however, the amount of time you invest into it is going to be one-week at the most. Prior to conducting any research, you need to have a clear set of questions that you want answered. The answers you get will dictate the way you have the executive sponsors deliver the message, how the message is designed, and the sequence (of how/in which) it actually flows to the impacted community of employees.

To get you going, focus on getting answers to the following questions:

- What pains employees most about this project?
- What are the common complaints from the group of people vocally resisting?
- Why is vocalizing this/these complaints so important?
- Who are the employees vocalizing (i.e., title, location, tenure, gender)?
- When did they start experiencing the problems creating the complaints?
- What would it take for resistors to become advocates?
- What are the patterns among the classes of groups (resistors, neutrals, advocates)?
- If the group of resistors could fix the situation with no limitations – how or what would they do?

As you approach the base to get your data, consider collecting it through brief surveys, key person interviews, and small focus groups. Given your tight timeline, remember, don't spend more than one-week on this part of the process. You need all the time you can get for the message delivery.

Build the candidate – You went through the process and notion of generating and gathering data to help you with the next part of the process – the part where you "build the candidate." The candidate in this scenario is going to be the product you are releasing. Think back to the Coca-Cola and Zappos commercials – their candidates were also their products. You are doing the same thing here.

Building a candidate needs the following special ingredients:

- ✓ Refined message + reason to believe: by now you should have a much more meaningful message, one derived from the golden nuggets of information given to you by the employees you interviewed during focus groups, demographic data, and survey research.

- ✓ Consistency: the message must be used in a consistent manner, it cannot- I repeat, it cannot be watered down with variations of the same message. Variations are good sometimes, but not for you--at least, not in this situation. In the present context. variations will simply create confusion.

- ✓ Repetition: your campaign will spread and when it does, focus on it being repeated in the same way (i.e., consistency). Especially, because it will be used by multiple key team members.

- ✓ Appearance and design: create a logo, slogan or tag line for the campaign. Try to make it something that employees can personalize, focus on making it something that they can also personify. Think of it this way, most people personify personal objects (cars, phones, laptops, etc.,) as well as pets – they do this by giving them cute or meaningful names. You need them to also personally identify with your campaign, the more they psychologically connect with it, the more emotionally invested they will be with it, which means that they will also be highly supportive of it.

Media – By now you have, a team in place, you have researched what your community of impacted employees care about, and you have crafted a meaningful message. Now, you can focus on using creative ways to spread the message of your campaign.

Keep in mind, every organization is different and they all have various policies on use of communication channels, media outlets, and social media. All that is to say, you might need to get some of your campaign items cleared by a marketing team or a similar group. This process is faster if you already have these people on your team from the very beginning. The key is to know who you need before they know that you need them. Be strategic.

Here are some common pathways you can use:

- o Media outlets
  - Emails and signature lines.
  - Corporate intranet (website or page dedicated to the project).
  - Digital boards, desktop backscreens.
  - Physical banners (recommended only when you have a healthy budget).
  - Small group meetings, roadshows, townhalls, corporate events.

o Type of content

- Executive sponsor(s) messaging (updates, roadblocks, milestones, accomplishments, etc.,).
- Influencers (promoting key ideas or features).
- Change agents (supporting the community).
- Experiential (street) team (creating happiness experiences around the product).
- Endorsers (evangelizing the value they have received by using product).

Here are some less traditional pathways to spread the message of your campaign.

o Take many photos of key people on the team doing specific things. Use photos over video for this, because still images force the receiver to create a personalized story in their minds. Here are some suggestions.

- Executive sponsor(s) with other corporate leaders using the product.
- Executive sponsors(s) visiting various types of departments of impacted employees.
- Executive sponsor(s) wearing shirts, hoodies, hats with logo or tag.
- Influencers wearing shirts (different colors in different locations) with the message on them.
- Change agents supporting staff with the use of the product.

- Change agents presenting content about the product at a new employee onboarding session.
- Endorsers meeting with tenured employees with the product in the background.
- Endorsers surrounded by change agents (include laughter in the image).

o Leak specific messages to arouse emotions.

o Create intentional debates and disagreements. Plant people in the audience of roadshows or small group meetings to challenge the path you are on. This will encourage people to "fight" for what they believe in (i.e., support the product). This one is tricky and you can only do it if you are certain that your campaign is moving strong.

Timeline – The last item on this list is for you to know when you should activate each element of your campaign strategy for "Initiative X." The timeline below (Table 8-3) is just one of several ways that you focus your efforts, given the quick turnaround requested by your client.

Initiative X Timeline			
Month 1	Month 2	Month 3	Month 4
• Identify and activate the core team. • Acknowledge failed attempt (light heartedly). • Conduct research. • Draft message.	• Refine message. • Design persona for your message. • Identify media outlets. • Purchase material needed for experiential (street) team. • Provide direction to corporate influencers.	• Activate executive sponsor messaging ("something good is coming"). • Run vague digital board ads.	• Activate executive sponsor roadshows. • Host townhall, small group meetings to promote the message. • Host "Initiative X" party. • Take photos and run photo ads every three days.

Table 8-3: Initiative x timeline

The visual below (Figure 8-3) depicts what you can expect to see by running a campaign such as this. Let me help you read this visual. The B.Y represents the work the client did (Before You), as you can see there are three specific outcomes called-out here: 1) they were doing good, then something happened and it moved to bad. 2) the strategy was boring so they got no movement. 3) they started-off on the wrong foot and evolved it to a stabilized format.

The big grey circle is you and the A.Y marker represents the work you put into place by joining the project (After You). Rest assured that it doesn't matter who you are and what you do, there will always be a natural decline after introducing something new, so don't get hung up on this–you will move past it. During the A.Y period you should be able to see movement and progress toward a new perception and awareness of "Initiative X." By the fourth month, all items within the campaign strategy you created should be activated and everyone is doing their part to kick things into gear. This is also where you can expect to see the highest level of achievement.

The T.Y marker represent a period in which you transition the work over to the client. The team should be able to run things on their own at this point. Just be mindful that the achievement you observed during month three and month four will also come with a small decline in month five and month six. Remind your client and the team that this is normal and expected. It is far more important for them to focus on how to bounce back from the decline as it begins to show up. The transition strategy you provide for your client will do one of two things for your client – it will either allow "Initiative X" to thrive– or, cause it to fall back down to a boring (or worse negative) state. Three possible client outcomes are displayed to the right of the T.Y marker on the visual. Either way, you are leaving the client in a better position.

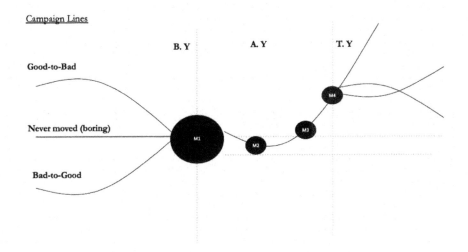

Figure 8-3: Campaign strategy lines

TECHNIQUE #2 – THE MESSAGE, THE CANDIDATE: SOMETHING TO BELIEVE IN

Political agendas have very specific agendas they want to push to the people. It is easy for someone to get behind (or against) a mission or a slogan when the person serving as the face for the message is one who is known, liked, or hated by the people. Remember, feelings of happiness, joy, laughter, frustration, anger, and hatred all create movements. Your goal is to create an emotional association between your executive sponsor and the message of your campaign.

This section is about combining a good campaign message with an ideal candidate, so that they can do what they are designed to do: which is to create a movement worth talking about.

A good campaign strategist knows the message that they need to convey to the general populous, they just need the "right" candidate to help them carry that message.

Let's explore this concept using the following political movements...

Who comes to mind when you read the following chant?

"Yes, we can!"

If you said, Barrack Obama, good job, but that's wrong. Well, okay fine, you are partially correct. The reason why you thought about Obama is because a crafty campaign manager recycled it from a union leader and social activist from the 1960's. You can't argue with a good message – all you need is the right candidate to help you exploit it.

The original chant ("Si se puede") came from Dolores Huerta a co-founder of the National Farm Workers of America. The other founder was Cesar Chavez, a big personality for the Latino community who also happened to be a big target base for the 2008 Obama political campaign. The beauty in this chant is that it was folded into Obama's much larger theme of hope and change. For the full history of the chant see the United Farm Worker's website under "history of si se puede."[45]

Let's try one more.

Who comes to mind when you read the following?

"Let's make America great again!"

If Donald J. Trump popped into your mind, you are close! Trump's actual slogan is "Make America Great Again" or MAGA for short.[46] Not to split hairs or anything, but it is argued that Trump was "inspired" from former president Ronald Regan's 1980 campaign. As I said before – a good message is a good message. If you are interested in learning more, go to YouTube to watch various clips and footage of the phrase being used.[47]

Let's transition our thought process back into the corporate setting.

So, how do you find or know that you have the ideal candidate to push the campaign's message?

Answering this can be a bit tricky but there is a process you can follow to make sure that things are in your favor during the turnaround campaign. This process is coupled with a list of four questions that you can ask to gauge the person's level of "ideal-ness."

Keep in mind that you will not have the luxury of going into a company and plucking an employee to help you push a turnaround campaign strategy. Instead, the likely scenario will be that you are pulled into a project by an executive who is struggling to create (or to recover) a movement for a particular project. Perhaps, you will get lucky and have the opportunity to select a co-sponsor.

Here's how I typically approach this situation ...

Step 1 – I start with a discovery conversation. There are four questions that I like to use when I need to groom the executive sponsor to become the ideal candidate for the campaign's message. I ask them the following questions.

1. Why are you involved with this project?
2. What qualifies you to lead this project and what sets you apart from someone else taking lead on this project?
3. How much time, effort, money, and reputation are you willing to invest into this project before you pull the plug?
4. What are the things getting in the way (or going to)?

Step 2 – the way they answer these questions will inform you on where and how much time you need to spend grooming them. I caution you to be skeptical of the answers they give you. Chances are that they will be short and not helpful whatsoever. This means that you have to take your time and guide them through the conversation. I like to be upfront and tell them that the more complete, authentic and comprehensive their answers are, the better I will be able to help them.

Step 3 – I study the answers the sponsor gives me and schedule two additional follow-up meetings, asking them the same exact questions (in a different sequence). This tells me how much and to what extend their answers change. It also gives me an insight into their tendency to ramble, innovate, back-peddle, or allow emotional states to dictate their responses. On occasions I video record our conversation (with their permission), so that they can see how others will see them and their responses. The last thing you need is for them to say different things to different people when you have them out doing roadshows, townhalls, and meetings with targeted employees.

In the event that you do not have the opportunity to have grooming sessions with the executive sponsor(s), you must do whatever you can do sit on the team that gives the executive advice. The client might tell you that they don't have such a thing, but trust me, there always is one or two people giving the executive advice – you need to be one of those people, so do what you can to keep the messaging and conversations in check. Otherwise, the message will be diluted or completely botched.

TECHNIQUE #3 – CHECK AND CONTROL YOUR T.I.M.P.

In this section you will learn about four vital elements of a campaign strategy. These elements were adapted from *The Political Campaign Desk Reference*,[41] where the author calls them irreplaceable campaign commodities. In my mind - as they relate to a turnaround plan - there is no way you can pull off a successful recovery without having all of these elements constantly flowing and alive. I even go as far as calling them the lifeline of any campaign, because without them, the whole thing falls apart and dies.

To help me remember them, I use the acronym T.I.M.P. It stands for:

- ✓ **Time:** this is equal to the amount of time that you have remaining or available to put tactics in place to make a recovery. For instance, four months to the technology implementation or ten days for the merger to close. Some people argue that you can simply push the go-live date, transition date, or closing date. True, this might allow you to inject a little more life into your project, but that is only temporary and at some point, you will lose the "patient" (i.e., impacted audience).

- ✓ **Information:** this relates to all aspects of a campaign. There is only so much information you can get from the target audience about making things better. There is a limited amount of content that you can push out to the impacted users about the greatness of your project. There is only so much attention anyone will be willing to give you.

- ✓ **Money:** this seems pretty simple to me. When you run out of money, you also run out of the ability to pay for the resources you need to keep the project alive.

✓ **People:** running out of any of these elements is bad, but losing the minds and hearts of the people is probably one of the worst things that can happen to any turnaround plan. As long as you have a small number of people who still believe in the project, it is still recoverable. However, the question you need to ask your client and yourself is – is it worth it? A recovery plan that has already lost the people takes an incredible amount of effort and investment on the T.I.M elements. There's nothing wrong with dropping the turnaround plan and preparing for the next project to make sure it is better executed.

As a technique, one of the first things I recommend for you to do when rolling-on to a new project is for you to do a pulse check on T.I.M.P. A quick assessment will tell you where you need to focus your time to bring the most value for your client. However, be cognizant that if you run out of any of them, that's it – it's over. Occasionally, you will be able to inject more of a particular element to increase the project's life, but at some-point not even that injection will help keep the project alive.

In an effort to prevent being blindsided, you can enforce the creation of a health dashboard. Make sure that your dashboard includes the T.I.M.P elements and that the team understands their meaning and value. Remember, you are all in this together!

Chapter Eight

Summary

In this chapter, you learned how to take a topic that people are not aware of and convert it into something that they talk about for months. Thinking like a campaign strategist teaches you to create a persona that people can relate to and learn to associate with. In other words, you learned that you can take a corporate "nobody" and make them into a corporate "somebody." This also applies to a failing project or when you are asked to help stabilize a crisis. Yes, you can do all of that by thinking like a campaign strategist.

This chapter provided you with some basic techniques used by campaign strategists, political consultants, media manipulators, and corporate advisors to create something out of nothing, and to lead corporate turnarounds.

Know this...there will be a time in the journey of your career as a turnaround specialist (i.e. a "fixer") when one of your clients will need you to think like a campaign strategist. This will likely happen as a result of your client wanting to kick-off a new project or venture to bring something positive. On the other hand, it can also result from something negative - like, a company having to react to a bad public relations issue.

Much like running a corporate turnaround strategy, a campaign strategy uses steps and action plans to create movement from the target community. By thinking like a campaign strategist, you learned techniques to create something out of nothing; to get people involved in the greater good.

CHAPTER NINE

THE LAWYER

"There is lots of my work that takes place behind closed doors that is not ever seen." ~ Amal Clooney

Many of us have seen television shows or movies where lawyers are depicted arguing a case to put away a bad guy, saving the day of a family in need, or protecting a giant corporation. For cinematic purposes the cases, scenes, and storylines are glorified and do not represent the full spectrum of the intensive detailed work that lawyers do to protect the rights and interests of their clients. I bet it wouldn't make for good viewer ratings to watch a lawyer sitting at their desk doing research, reading case law, writing summary statements or creating recommendations to present to the client.

Before writing this chapter, I had a general understanding of what lawyers do within their practice to best serve the interests of their clients. However, it was through research and interviews that I was able to get a deeper appreciation and respect for the profession and the critical role that its practitioners play in protecting people-from-people.

The sad reality is that just as much as our world has nice, kind, and loving people – it has just as many jerks looking to do intentional harm and take advantage of others. This reality breeds the necessity of having a system in place to protect people-from-people. We all need (or will need) the help of a lawyer at some point in our lives. There is a lawyer for virtually every problem you can think of. This chapter will not get into the intricacies of all of types of lawyers – you don't need that (at least not for now).

This chapter will however, provide you with some general ways of viewing the world that I have learned by studying and interviewing lawyers. The perspectives I am sharing with you have been useful when helping clients get a project back on its feet.

Just in case it's not clear, I am not providing you with legal advice nor am I pretending to be a lawyer– and neither should you (unless, you are one, in which case – keep up the good work!).

For those of you interested in learning more about the complexities of the lawyer profession, I recommend an introductory article titled – *Types of Lawyers* - by Belle Wong, J. D., a freelance contributing writer for LegalZoom (an internet company that makes legal help more widely accessible). In her article, Belle provides an overview of the many types of lawyers in the market and the specialties they serve to help clients deal with very specific situations.[48]

The umbrella of the lawyer profession is very wide and complex, so this chapter will not get into the details of trying to explain what the various types of lawyers do nor the many techniques that they use. Instead, this chapter will provide you with three key ways of viewing the world that are common across many types of lawyers in the legal profession. I encourage you to use these perspectives as a springboard to help you craft strategic turnaround plans for your clients by seeing the world through the lens of a lawyer.

The Lawyer Perspective	
Common areas to apply this perspective	<ul><li>Strategic planning</li><li>Culture transformations (mergers, acquisitions, divestitures)</li><li>Organizational design (restructures, workforce reductions)</li><li>Growth strategies</li><li>Scalability modeling (typical of start-up companies)</li></ul>
Qualities of people in this field	<ul><li>Deductive and inductive reasoning</li><li>Risk mitigator</li><li>Resourceful</li><li>Networking skills</li><li>Perseverance</li></ul>

Table 9-1: The lawyer perspective

WHY SHOULD I THINK LIKE A LAWYER?

Thinking like a lawyer will challenge your current way of seeing the world. It will force you to stretch your mind, to be more strategic in your approach to client solutions, to anticipate possible outcomes by using multiple points of view, and to grow your resourcefulness by finding creative ways to stack the odds in your client's favor.

Thinking like a lawyer will encourage you to appreciate the perspective of others, even when you completely disagree with that particular perspective – heck, thinking like a lawyer will also help you argue with logic and reason in favor of that perspective.

In the campaign strategist chapter, I mentioned that you need to leverage emotions to help you drive momentum, change, and recovery. Well, in this chapter, I am here to tell you that running on emotions and making decisions based on them is bad for business. Such a contradiction, I know– but hear me out. Thinking like a lawyer helps you use logic and reason to plot the best course of action for your clients.

Word of advice, emotions will find their way into your practice, don't try to suppress them or try to ignore them. There is a significant difference between managing emotions and suppressing them – one is bad for your mental and physical health. Instead of suppressing your charged emotions, see them as a temporary hungry cookie monster within your headspace. The monster (your emotions) will eat all of your cookies, until you stop feeding them. By simply knowing they are around and hungry (the key being to not feed them), they will go away on their own. Use the mindfulness techniques you learned in chapter two to help keep your cool.

By reading, internalizing, and applying the views of this chapter, my hope is that you will have more tools under your belt to help your clients revitalize a failing situation.

THE TRANSFORMATION MODEL

To revitalize a project, you should be prepared for the very real possibility that people (this can include your client) will lie to you, people will keep things from you, and people get in the way even if it means sabotaging their own plan. Don't get me wrong, not all people, clients, or situations will turn out this way. There is a bright side, one where you will have the delightful pleasure of working with amazing people who will do everything within their means to improve themselves and the situation. As you read on, you will find that the majority of your efforts when thinking like a lawyer will involve the "barriers" element of the transformation model (Figure 9-1).

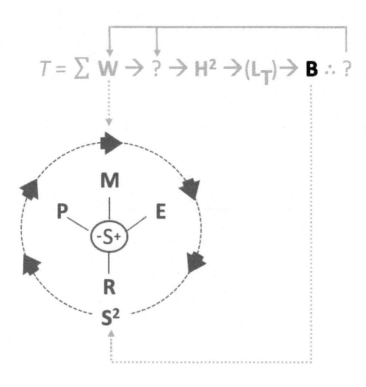

Figure 9-1: The transformation model

As a refresher:

> **B** stands for "Barriers or Blockers."
>
> These are the things that **_will_** get in the way of the situation turning around. Focus on identifying them quickly (or even better – be able to anticipate them), so that you can create recovery plans.
>
> I encourage you to keep your eye on people (emotions, behaviors, patterns) and processes (ways of doing things or not doing them) type barriers. I have found them to be a pain-in-

the-ass throughout my journeys with failing projects. When you run into these barriers be cautious that they often come as a pair, meaning when there is a process-problem there usually is a people-problem, and vice versa.

One more thing: you will quickly realize that every business objective comes with a hidden personal objective. Use your skills by thinking like a psychologist (from chapter 3) to find the hidden personal value tied to the business objective.

For example:

By the Head of Human Resources	
Business objective (verbally stated)	**Personal objective** (quietly hoping for)
We want to create alignment, effective communication, and teamwork amongst the leadership team.	Help me! I'm tired of babysitting and intervening this group of people.

In the following section a business challenge is presented, describing a common scenario where it will be helpful for you to think like a lawyer. The challenge is followed by a "view of the world" section, which details an approach, insight, or technique designed to help you solve the presenting challenge. Keep in mind, the challenges presented along with the views of the world are simplified for illustrative purposes. The goal here is for you to expand your thinking and incorporate different views within your approach, instead of having a one-size fits all solution.

Let's begin…

> ▶ **Business Challenge: What the Future Holds (Strategic Planning)**

THE CLIENT:

The client is a not-for-profit organization focused on helping middle school kids in the surrounding communities gain leadership and entrepreneurial skills. The mission of this company (let's give the company a fake name - FewTure) is to prepare the youth for the future workforce by teaching them foundational skills related to management (i.e., social skills), running a business (i.e., balancing a checkbook), and work-life balance (i.e., mental, physical, emotional health skills).

THE CURRENT SITUATION:

FewTure, is relatively new to the market, they have been around for six years. In their short existence, they have been able to gain a reputation as a company that truly cares, which has allowed them the opportunity to continuously secure a decent amount of funding from generous donors and sponsors. At present day, they are managing a purse of 2 million dollars that allows them to keep the lights on in the business while also keeping the kids in the program actively engaged. Although, they are doing good for themselves, the board of directors would like for FewTure to do more. They are putting pressure on the Executive Director to expand their outreach to include high school kids, and to also open a sister center across town. According to the board, high school kids would benefit more and FewTure would make a greater impact to the surrounding community by focusing on kids who will be entering the workforce soon (as compared to their current base target - the middle school kids).

HERE'S WHAT YOU KNOW:

In an effort to appease the board of directors and to get additional funding, the executive director and his team put a strategic plan in place. The plan was designed to come to life over the course of three-years with key milestones at the one, two, and three-year marker. They are currently toward the end of their first year, which means that they are already behind schedule.

The plan was designed to accomplish the following goals (items not listed in any particular order):

- Open a second center across town (current status: yellow).
- Expand their market and services to high school kids (current status: yellow).
- Review, revise, and update the learning curriculum (current status: red).
- Increase the number of volunteers to support the expected growth and demands (current status: red).

- Recruit additional staff to support the expected growth and demands (current status: red).
- Secure additional funding to pay for everything (current status: red).

THE CHALLENGE (YOUR INVOLVEMENT):

The Executive Director called you in because he is freaking out and constantly on edge. He gives you a laundry list of problems and reasons why their plan is failing.

Here's what you uncover...

- they are obviously behind schedule;
- the team is not getting along (they are constantly bickering and fighting with each other);
- volunteers are not showing-up when they are supposed to or are dropping entirely;
- money is being spent at an alarming rate and no new funding is coming in to replace it.

The list goes on with other challenges, but this gives us enough information to play with.

Now, we can get into how you can help your client turn this situation around by viewing the world like a lawyer.

VIEW OF THE WORLD #1 – IDAC

IDAC is an acronym that stands for: Issue, Details, Analysis, Conclusion. It is an approach inspired by the acronym – IRAC[49] – which is one of many– and I mean many– acronyms used by law students when they are learning how to think like a lawyer. It stands for: Issue, Rule, Analysis, Conclusion. If you are interested in learning more about this method, hop over to LawNerds.com and search for IRAC Formula.[50] You will find that it is a pragmatic, logical, and tactical way of approaching a case. Since, we are not in the legal game – our goal is to use similar logic to help our clients get back on track.

Let's dig in and apply it to our strategic plan scenario.

ISSUE:

> The client says the issue is simple: they are behind on the timeline. He says "all we need is a workshop on time management skills and communicating effectively – that should get us back on track."

> Clearly, you know this won't solve anything – you also pick up on his stress level. So, you leverage your chapter 3 (thinking like a psychologist) skills to help calm him down and your chapter 4 (thinking like an investigator) skills to get more details on the presenting problem, before you make any recommendations or create any recovery plans.

DETAILS:

You engage the client on a series of open-ended questions to help you get crisp on the details of the problem. These questions are designed to help you get a better sense of how the client got to the current state and what it would take for them to recover from it.

To speed things up, I am presenting the question and providing an answer.

Your Question: How did things get to where they are now?

> **Client Response:** I feel like we are all running around going in multiple directions pressed for time, but yet we are not getting anywhere and we have the same conversations over and over during our meetings.

Your Question: Which of the problems pains you the most?

> **Client Response:** I hate that we don't have a location for our next center. I don't get why it is taking so long to find it.

Your Question: Anything else?

> **Client Response:** It would be nice if we knew where our money is being spent. We were doing fine when I was in charge of the books, but now it seems like we have a mountain of receipts and expenses to go with them.

Your Question: Anything else?

Client Response: Hmmm, we are having a difficult time helping the community see the future, it's so bright and great, but they just don't get it. I wish they could listen to our board of directors talk about the great things we want to do for our kids.

Your Question: What would it take for these problems to go away?

Client Response: People just need to focus and do their job. It's that simple – well, at least in my eyes, it's that simple.

ANALYSIS:

After some back and forth open-ended dialogue you have a better picture of your client's underlying problem. Now, you can target key areas to alleviate the pain they are experiencing.

By paying attention to the details of what your client said during your conversation you would have picked up on the following things.

Client Themes	Your Analysis
…running around … multiple directions… not getting anywhere… same conversations …	• Lack of roles and responsibilities
…I don't get why…	• Poor organizational structure
…when I was in charge of the books…	• Unclear deliverables mapped to timeline
…I wish they could listen to our board…in my eyes…	• Could use a campaign strategy

CONCLUSION:

As you can see, there were plenty of emotions at play here, but you kept your cool, stayed objective, and were able to see the details underlying the presenting concerns. The client obviously has many issues, don't get fooled into thinking that you need to have a solution for all of them. Often times, by simply focusing on a few main areas, you are able to chip away at the other issues without even trying.

Here's how you were able to help your client gain traction and to get their strategic plan and timeline back on track.

✓ You sat with the executive director and his team to co-create an organizational structure (think a boxes and sticks diagram). The idea behind this is to allow the space for them to align on who is doing what and by when. It seems that the executive director was wearing multiple hats (like the old days when he first launched the company), but in the process of growing he forgot to delegate tasks and responsibilities. In other words, he metaphorically passed the baton, but there was no one there to take it, because they didn't know they had to be there.

✓ After structuring the new organizational design, everyone is now clear on who is responsible for managing the funds. Just because the executive director did it at first, it does not mean that he should continue to do it, nor does it mean that he is the right person for the job. This stopped the financial bleeding and allowed the fund committee to focus on generating new cash-flow.

✓ A campaign strategy was put in place to drive movement amongst the community, increase volunteer involvement, and re-establish gifting donations. The board of directors got involved by doing speaking engagements and spreading the word of what the future holds.

► Business Challenge: Growing Pains (Scalability Modeling)

THE CLIENT:

The client is a small company servicing the events industry. Let's give them a fake name of "Events-for-All." This company focuses on managing and planning events for weddings, corporate parties, and professional conferences. "Events-for-All" was started by four friends who met each other through course of bumping into one-another at various events they were hosting. Each one of them had an independent solo practice of their own and decided to join forces to create one larger company. When they started it was just the four of them focusing on different aspects of the business (i.e., photography/videography, music/entertainment, catering, vendor management/planning) and they have grown the company to 25 employees with a mix of subcontractors in the span of 18-months.

THE CURRENT SITUATION:

The client wants to get into other segments of their market and offer additional services. They also want to build a custom online application to help them manage their tasks. Lastly, they want to grow the company to be 2x's what it is today. According to the partners, Events-for-All plans to double their staff size to be at 50+ employees, so that they can take on more clients and generate more business. Figure 9-2, shows a simple visual of their desired goal.

Figure 9-2: The client goal

Events-for-All was sent your way by a start-up company that you provided strategic advice on how to scale their business. Events-for-All heard what you did and they want you to help them do the same for their company.

Seems reasonable, right?

Keep reading…

HERE'S WHAT YOU KNOW:

Before you came into the picture, the partners already started working on a scalability plan to grow their staff. One of the partners even created marketing material to break into hosting "experiential events" for corporations. The landing page of their promo ad highlights the great features of using "Events-for-All" for a corporate training retreat.

They put their heads together and created a three-prong plan to be split amongst the four of them (interesting math, but okay).

Their plan includes the following business objectives (hint: remember there are likely hidden personal objectives to go along with these):

- Grow number of employees.
  - Each partner is required to invest an additional $20,000 to fund the headcount.
  - Each partner is required to recruit friends and family to join the company.
  - Expand their service portfolio to include "experiential events."
  - Contract a platform developer to custom build an event planner platform to manage all of their growing needs.

THE CHALLENGE (YOUR INVOLVEMENT):

One of the partners calls you because he wants you to meet with the four of them to take a look at their plan and provide them with some quick-tips or "stuff" to look for as they go on with their journey.

Normally, you wouldn't take a case who wants "tips" on "stuff" – but the referral came from a good client of yours, so you take a courtesy meeting with them.

Through the discovery conversation you uncover that all of the partners are very interested and invested in the idea of adding more employees. You find it odd that they are stuck on this idea, so you go on with the conversation. You also uncover that they like to be part of the lifecycle of their service process: they like to have conversations with clients, and want to negotiate the best price from vendors and subcontractors. They also very much enjoy attending the events they put on to see everything come to life (hint – I bet this is a personal hidden objective).

At the end of the conversation, one of the partners says: "so, what do you think – any tips?"

After you throw-up in your mouth a little (figuratively speaking, of course) and compose yourself. You tell them…

"No, I don't have any "tips" on "stuff" for you, but if you are really serious about scaling your business, I can help you with that. It will require you to think differently from your current approach."

They take you up on the offer and you get to work.

VIEW OF THE WORLD # 2 – DO YOU SEE WHAT I SEE?

I have learned from studying and researching lawyers that anyone can argue their own personal point of view. It's easy, because all they are doing is using their personal beliefs, schemas of the world, and emotions to drive their convictions.

On the other hand, a really good lawyer can argue for or against anything in a persuasive manner. This is because they can see things from multiple perspectives and they don't let emotions cloud their judgement. There is a misconception that lawyers should not be emotional. I have found that really good lawyers are able to flex their emotions to channel their passion to drive empathy and sympathy from their audience (regardless of their own personal beliefs about the situation). They are persuasive because they help people see things from different positions, which is exactly the approach you want to take with this client. The goal is for the client to remove their emotional investment and to instead apply logic, strategy, and reason to accomplish their business objectives.

At the moment, the four partners believe that growth is directly correlated with the number of people they have working for them, which explains why they want to double in size. This sounds logical, but it is not very strategic, because with the increase in people also comes an increase in cost and exposure to risk. So, you have to get the client to see things from a different point of view. This can be tricky, because they have so much emotion invested into their idea – they may be offended when you ask them to drop their view.

You approach this problem by using a line of questioning inspired by the Socratic Method, which is essentially a strategy to help your client redirect their focus.

You ask them the following questions. For simplicity, only the questions are presented below.

1. How are you performing financially?
2. What is (are) your most profitable area(s) of service?
3. Who among you is developing new business (i.e., who is selling the work)? And how?
4. Who will develop business for the new service you want to offer? And how?

5. Who is doing the hands-on work?

6. Who is managing the current staff?

7. How will the new people be managed? What is HR's involvement?

8. What are you doing about the legal and tax implications that comes with growing your headcount?

Through this line of questioning, the client begins to see several flaws in their approach. You helped them see...

- They can drop one of the services, because it is costing them a lot of money to keep it alive.

- All partners are spending their time doing manual (time consuming) work, instead of developing new business.

- The company doesn't have a proper HR person or department, and was not aware that they are opening themselves to more risks associated with tax and legal implications by increasing the size of their staff. They also just learned that one of their employees is pregnant and they don't know what to do about her upcoming leave of absence.

The upside is that the client did not get far enough with their original idea to need a full-blown recovery plan, instead your goal is more of a strategic realignment. The downside is that partners feel emotionally deflated—but the good news is, you can work with that.

1. To target growth and scalability, you work with the client to focus and commit to a new set of business objectives (which you tied to a timeline).

2. Focus their energy and resources on enhancing the highest performing services.

3. The partners stop doing the work that is not critical to business development. They focus their time throughout the day on meeting with prospective clients. They must trust that their people can do the work.

4. They create career journeys (development plans) for the current staff, in an effort to plan for them to stay with the company for a long time.

5. Instead of each of partner investing $20,000 into hiring more people, the money is used to...

   a. Purchase an affordable online solution to manage events and tasks. Instead of building one from scratch that would have easily cost them $100,000+.

   b. All tasks and business operations that are not directly adding value to the bottom line and are sucking up time from business development are outsource or automated (e.g., HR tasks can be outsourced and managed by a professional firm).

By targeting these key areas, your client was able to reduce operational waste and eliminate unnecessary costs, which contributed to them making substantially more money. Your client was eventually able to expand their employee count which also enabled them to expand their service offerings. In other words, you were able to help them grow and scale, and you did it by helping them see things from multiple points of view.

Business Challenge: Creating A Family (Culture Transformation)

THE CLIENT:

The client is a private language school headquartered in France with several satellite locations across Europe and the Americas. Let's give them a fake name of "L'ecole" (French for "the school"). In recent months (before you joined the project), the leadership team attended a strategic planning summit, where they drafted a vision for the next six years. Their plan is to become the world's elite language school. To reach that goal they came-up with the "Three Pillars of Transformation" (Figure 9-3).

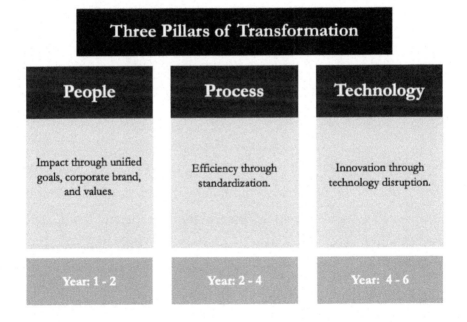

Figure 9-3: The three pillars of transformation

THE CURRENT SITUATION:

This transformation project is scheduled to advance in phases by year and by departmental leaders. The three leaders will collaborate across the entire lifecycle of the project, but each phase represents a different level of responsibility for each of the assigned leaders. For example, year 1 – 2 is under the leadership of the VP of Global Strategy, then year 2 – 4 is handed over to the VP of Global Business Operations (i.e., the Lean Optimization Team), with a final transition over year 4 – 6 to the VP of Global Technology.

The Vice President of Global Strategy calls you because she needs your help getting this project back on track. She and her team of internal consultants have been working on this initiative for the past six months, but things are not going the way they expected them to, and she is starting to get the feeling that she will miss her year-end target. According to the VP, they have plans in action, but something is missing, because her teams keeps having the same resistance roadblocks by the employees.

She informs you that she is meeting once again with the Marketing team to create another version of the already new branding identify. This time they want to have the brand highlight the fact that L'ecole and its employees are a family and are in this transformation together. They also have plans to work with the HR team to redesign the current onboarding program. The strategy team believes that it is a good idea to have new hires become ambassadors for this culture transformation. The thought is that as newly minted ambassadors, new hires will be able to spread the word about the vision and get others to join the movement, as a family.

THE CHALLENGE (YOUR INVOLVEMENT):

You meet with the VP of Strategy to get the specifics on what she needs your help with. At this time, you are going to leverage your skills to think like a diagnostician (chapter 6) to understand her pain points. Basically, you are coming in to say – show me where it hurts.

HERE'S WHAT YOU KNOW:

During this conversation the VP informs you of the following:

The Global Executive Committee gave your client (the VP of Strategy) three business objectives.

1. Create a new unified corporate brand. This should be consistent across all locations.
2. Start the conversation of centralizing business processes (this sets the path for the VP of Operations to take over). This should be done by establishing global business goals that all departments and schools can follow. This includes the new acquisitions happening throughout the year.
3. Update the corporate values to reflect their new strategic direction of become a global elite language school.

As of six months into the project, your client has done the following.

- Created a new brand identity.

- o Problem with this – the client is having trouble making it stick with the employees.

- A campaign was created and launched to promote the new corporate values.
  - o Problem with this – same as above, people in the organization are not fully aware or involved.

- New hires go through the new onboarding program and are required to act as ambassadors.
  - o Problem with this – the culture transformation stops with new hires, because they are new, and have no connections or ideas on how to spread the word.

As you get deeper into the conversation and she tells you where it hurts, you uncover the following:

- The strategy team is composed of a project manager, a business operations person, a strategy person and a few junior analysts. Her team is missing a change management person, a trainer, a communications person, and a set of corporate influencers.
- The strategy team never conducted a culture organizational assessment to get a baseline of current values, belief systems, or displayed corporate behaviors.
- The strategy team is not aware of what the current employee engagement scores are or if an action plan was ever created to increase engagement scores.

- The VP of Strategy was not planning on being part of any campaigns, instead she was giving the team full autonomy to do what they felt was right.
- There are no executives, leaders, or managers involved in spreading the word.

The list of uncovered issues has many more items, but you don't have time to work on all of them, so we will limit the list to the items mentioned above.

After your conversation with the client, you have a better sense of where the problems are, and now you need some ideas to experiment with. One of which is to start thinking like a lawyer: to open your mind and see solutions from multiple possible angles. You are aware that in order to help your client turn this situation around you need to be creative and resourceful with your solution.

VIEW OF THE WORLD #3 – CREATIVITY AND RESOURCEFULNESS

Thinking like a lawyer requires you to have the ability to be creative and resourceful in your practice. Often times, lawyers find themselves in what seem like a "no-win" situation and are pressured by their clients to find a way out of that situation.

Don't worry, your client is not putting you in a box and closing-in the walls on you (well, at least not in this scenario). However, your client does feel like she is in a "no-win" situation herself and is coming to you for help. Your goal is to get your creative juices flowing to help her get back on track by implementing a clever solution to overcome her team's difficulties.

Let's jump into a recovery solution for this scenario using the steps presented in table 9-1. The first two-steps are self-explanatory, so we won't spend time on those and will instead focus on the last step of the process.

Step	Action
1	Add these players to the team. • Executive committee: (composed of the three VP's, directors, and managers) • Change management lead • Communication specialist • Corporate influencers • Social media shadows • Trainer
2	Have the strategy team review and analyze current data on values and employee engagement to create a baseline to measure against as the project continues.
3	Release the "shock and recovery plan." This is where you leverage your creativity and resourcefulness to get the project back on track.

Table 9-1: The three-step action plan

Since you are thinking creatively like a lawyer, you know that you need to harness the momentum created from the resistance that employees are projecting toward this project. So, you decide to introduce shock into the symptoms of the organism (i.e., the company).

Stay with me…

As an expert in creating transformations you already know that organizations have a collective heartbeat that changes in rhythm based on internal and external forces placed upon it throughout the year. For illustrative purposes, imagine that L'ecole's heartbeat looks something like this (Figure 9-4).

Figure 9-4: Organizational heartbeat

Your plan is to introduce arrhythmia across key points throughout this phase of the culture transformation project. The goal is to establish a new organizational heartbeat based on the desired culture transformation. The changes will be done at three points along the journey (represented by M1, M2, M3 in Figure 9-5). Note, different clients will have different versions of the heartbeat – you must first understand its rhythm before you make any changes.

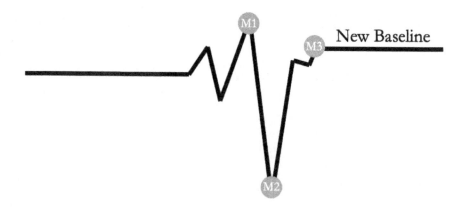

Figure 9-5: New baseline organizational heartbeat

To create changes, you introduce irregularities by implementing shock (M1), which is then followed by recovery (M2 – M3). The following image (Figure 9-5) is a visual representation of what your plan could look like for this particular client.

* * *

Word of advice, not all clients will be comfortable with the specific shock approach I am sharing with you – and it might not work as well with a large organization (1,000 + people). However, the concept of shock can be introduced in a less chaotic manner– the key is for you to work with your client on a creative solution that works best for them.

* * *

Figure 9-5: Shock and recover approach

It looks complicated, but it is actually very simple. Let's walk through it.

Shock (represented as M1) is introduced by having the highest-level leader (like a CEO, Founder, President, etc.) communicate something drastic to the workforce.

For this client you decide to go with your "You're fired" campaign strategy, in which the leader sends an email with a video explaining how everyone is fired (figuratively of course) including herself/himself. The video is intended to introduce shock (it's not a message you expect to get when you walk into work), which will set the impression and engagement rates on this campaign to go through the roof.

In the message, the leader talks about the journey to become a global elite language school – for that to happen they must leave behind all things that will get in the way. The only way to accomplish this goal is if it is done together – as a family. The video ends with a very specific transformation call-to-action plan (represented by M2 – M3).

After the video is released, it will take approximately 2 – 3 days for the full effect to take place across the organization. During this waiting period, there will be chatter, anxiety, and maybe even some crisis. Remember, people don't change when things are going well because they have no reason to do things differently. This is why crisis precipitates change.

During the 1 – 2 days of waiting, the marketing team releases more details on the "call-to-action" campaign where all employees are tasked with working together to create the future. The campaign highlights that key executives are leading the journey and will be visiting all locations to spread the message (represented as the ES diamond: "executive shows" in the visual).

On day three, executives begin their journeys and talk about a coalition group specifically designed to help "hire" everyone into the new company. At which point the executive team makes a transition over to the coalition team (M1 – M2).

The coalition team (composed of the roles in step one in table 9-1 and represented as the CS diamond: "coalition shows" in the visual), is charged with onboarding all employees into the "new company." This will take about four-weeks to complete (depending on size of organization).

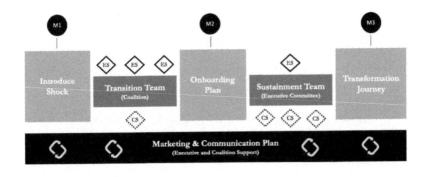

* * *

Word of advice, don't over complicate the onboarding process. It can be simple, meaningful, and impactful all at the same time. I do want to point out that the drop from M1 to M2 is going to be psychological, emotional, and financial. You can't expect to introduce a major change without it impacting the bottom line. Not to worry, it's predictable and recoverable.

* * *

While the coalition team is onboarding all employees, the marketing team continues to push hard on the culture transformation campaign (hosting townhalls, networking events, parties, etc.).

As the coalition team nears the end of the onboarding plan, the executives rejoin the campaign and are partnered with corporate influencers. This time the objective is to create sustainability (M2 → M3). The final piece is a transformation element, which is a set of roadshows and events that repeat on a monthly cadence to continuously reinforce behaviors. The transformation element can last anywhere between six-to-nine months, anything longer than that will lose value. Let's assume you run a nine-month block; you can begin to shift the project to the next VP starting at month seven – this will make it a smoother transition from one leader to the next.

By thinking creatively like a lawyer, you were able to help your client break away from her perceived idea of being stuck in a - no-win - situation. Your unconventional approach and use of resources helped her create a movement of change among the employees. The involvement of all key leaders allowed the messaging to stick and the implementation of a coalition team helped solidify new practices (values and business processes) that could be standardized across the globe. Your client was happy with your work and asked to keep you on a retainer, because your advice helps her see things from multiple points of view and you challenge her to think differently about situations.

Chapter Nine

Summary

In this chapter, you learned that thinking like a lawyer involves a logical, precise, creative, and resourceful level of thinking.

Thinking this way challenges your mind to find creative solutions to get a failing project back on track. Lawyers are said to embody key qualities (some of which are listed below) that enable them to anticipate a variety of possible outcomes by seeing the world in different ways.

- Deductive and inductive reasoning
- Risk mitigation
- Resourcefulness
- Perseverance

Thinking like a lawyer doesn't meant that you have to force someone into submission by having them see things your way. Instead, it should encourage you to appreciate the perspective of others, even when you find yourself in disagreement with their point of view.

By reading the views in this chapter, I hope that you are able to create and internalize new ideas of your own. Ideas that you can begin to apply on a daily basis throughout your life and personal career. My hope is that you have another view of the world and another set of mental tools to help you and your clients revitalize a failing situation.

CHAPTER TEN

CONCLUDING THOUGHTS
BRINGING IT ALL TOGETHER

I wrote this book to provide you with a less traditional path to creating transformations and finding ways to recover when things are falling apart. Throughout your journey reading this book, you learned that situations go on a declining path for many reasons. I don't know about you, but I have found that many of the situations I am asked to revitalize are related to people problems, which usually come to life as a result of unresolved conflicts, hidden personal agendas, insecurities, fears, and projections - just to name a few. I admit, the process can be emotionally and mentally draining, so it is helpful to have a model to work with, something to get you thinking about key elements to leverage through the transformation process.

By having you learn about the Transformation Model and all of the elements that go into making it work, it is my hope that you have been equipped with new tools, tactics, and techniques to help guide you through challenging situations you will encounter at work and in life . As you continue along your own journey and find yourself in a situation where a change or transformation must be created, I encourage you to refer back to part-one of this book and explore the elements of the Transformation Model. Think of the Transformation Model as a map. It will help you find your way back to your desired path; you will find that over time, the more you use the model the more intuitive it becomes and your strategies to help clients through change will be a natural part of the way you approach life.

In other words, The Transformation Model becomes a way of life for you and a mental model that guides your client through a process of getting situations back on track.

Applying the model can be as simple as getting the answers to these questions:

- What do you want to accomplish?
- Why do you want this/why is this important?
- How will you know we have accomplished this goal (what's the measure)?
- How much time do we have?
- What are things that will get in the way?
- Are you willing to do what I ask of you and to provide the needed support to get this done?

As you begin to apply the Transformation Model across your initiatives, I encourage you to challenge your perspective on the situations you are presented with by finding ways to think differently about the recovery plans you craft for your clients. There will be times when the solution to a problem doesn't come easy to you, so finding a solution will require that you see the world around you through different lenses. This is where part-two of this book introduced you to different perspectives and ways of seeing the world. Just imagine these professionals sitting at your round table, helping you to think of different ways to revitalize failing situations.

By now you have read through all the chapters, and have learned many ways that you can approach a situation and inject techniques to bring it back to life. Keep in mind, there are tons of books and consultant best practice guides that teach you how to implement a project from beginning-to-end. That's not what we focused on here, instead, the things you learned in this book were presented to advance your thinking and to enhance the skills you learned from those other books.

The next time you are asked to join a project to "fix" a situation, ask yourself – what is the situation really about? What perspective should I leverage to turn this back around? Use that as a starting point to visualize the various professionals and their perspectives you learned about in this book. It's helpful to take the time to visualize them in your mind (as if you are all part of the round table).

Imagine yourself looking to your left where you see…

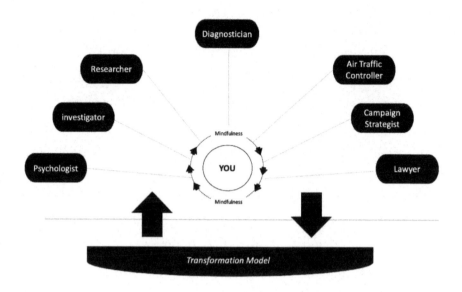

Figure 10-1: The round table realized

The psychologist: the perspective you activate when you need a psychological approach. Thinking like a psychologist grants you a deeper understanding of your clients by paying attention to their (expressed and hidden) needs.

The investigator: the perspective you leverage when you need to investigate a situation, while taking detailed notes and making unbiased observations. Thinking like an investigator allows you to remain objective and clear within your approach.

The researcher: the perspective you use when you need to experiment with ideas and test possible alternative solutions with rigor, logic, and science.

The diagnostician: the perspective you bring forth when the client provides you with a long list of presenting problems and their perceived solution to the problems. It is more likely that problems are merely symptoms of something else. Thinking like a diagnostician helps you to become more aware of underlying patterns and issues at play.

The air traffic controller: the perspective you use when you need help managing a ridiculous number of tasks, activities, and people. All while showing value, ROI, and KPI's to your client. Thinking like an air traffic controller helps you to take advantage of utilizing all possible resources, because after all time is money.

The campaign strategist: the perspective you put into action when you need to create something out of nothing. Thinking like a campaign strategist teaches you to create meaning and value, to create a turnaround strategy that inspires people to rally around the greater good (even one of a failing project).

The lawyer: the perspective you activate when you want your solutions to be precise, creative, and resourceful. This view challenges your mind to find creative solutions to get a situation back on track. Sometimes you will find yourself flipping your solutions upside down or putting them up to the light to see them in different angles. Thinking like a lawyer helps you to appreciate multiple points of view, to be creative, and resourceful in your solutions.

By reading this book, my hope is that you have expanded your view of the world and are able to create new ideas. Ideas that you can use and apply throughout your life and professional career. As you go off into the world, remember what you learned, and use your new skills to leave your client in a better condition than what you found them.

As a concluding thought, know that in this line of work, you will be called "the fixer, the turnaround specialist, or the revitalizer" – whatever you call it, I like to think that we are doing more than fixing a problem. I choose to believe that we are putting humans first, we are listening to the needs of the human condition, we are paying attention to the details of the things people say or the things they try to hide from us. It is our duty and responsibility to help them and to look out for their best interest.

Thank you for coming along with me on this journey!

REFERENCES

1. Kabat-Zinn, J. (1994). *Wherever You Go There You Are.* Hyperion, New York

2. Tan, C. (2012). *Search inside yourself: The unexpected path to achieving success, happiness (and world peace).* New York: Harper One.

3. Viktor E. Frankl Quotes. (n.d.). BrainyQuote.com. Retrieved July 5, 2019, from BrainyQuote.com Web site: https://www.brainyquote.com/quotes/viktor_e_frankl_160380

4. Be You Fully. (2016, July 16). *Empathic Listening, Carl Rogers* [Video file]. Retrieved from https://youtu.be/2dLsgpHw5x0

5. Beck, J. S. (2011), *Cognitive behavior therapy: Basics and beyond* (2nd ed.), New York, NY: The Guilford Press.

6. Maslow, A. (1954). *Motivation and Personality.* NY: Harper.

7. Piaget, J. (1958). The growth of logical thinking from childhood to adolescence. *AMC, 10, 12.*

8. Ellis, A. (1961). *A Guide to Rational Living.* Englewood Cliffs, N.J., Prentice-Hall.

9. Ajzen, I. (1985). The theory of planned behavior. Organizational Behavior and Human Decision Processes, 50, 179-211.

10. Rogers, C. (1951). *Client-centered therapy: Its current practice, implications and theory*. London: Constable.

11. Deci, E. L., & Ryan, R. M. (2000). The 'what' and 'why' of goal pursuits: Human needs and the self-determination of behavior. *Psychological Inquiry, 11*, 227-268.

12. Rigby, C. S., & Ryan, R. M. (2018). Self-determination theory in human resource development: New directions and practical considerations. *Advances in Developing Human Resources, 20(2)*, 133-147. doi: 10.1177/1523422318756954

13. Lutz, L., (n.d.). BrainyQuote.com. Retrieved July 5, 2019, from BrainyQuote.com: https://www.brainyquote.com/quotes/lisa_lutz_833254

14. Gene Luen Yang Quotes. (n.d.). BrainyQuote.com. Retrieved June 17, 2019, from BrainyQuote.com: https://www.brainyquote.com/quotes/gene_luen_yang_72640 9

15. Mashihi, S., Nowack, K., (2011), *Clueless: Coaching People Who Just Don't Get It*, Envisia Learning Inc.

16. Salkind, N. J. (2010). *Encyclopedia of research design* Thousand Oaks, CA: SAGE Publications, Inc. doi: 10.4135/9781412961288

17. Watkins, M. (2003). The first 90 days: Critical success strategies for new leaders at all levels. Boston, MA: Harvard Business School Press.

18. Wrisberg, Craig & M. Cassidy, Camille & K. Morgan, Taryn & Leanne Cherry, H. (2019). Naturalistic observations in sport and physical activity settings.

19. Kotter, J. P. (2012). *Leading change.* Cam- bridge, MA: Harvard Business Review Press.

20. Sloan., A. P., (n.d.). BrainyQuote.com. Retrieved May 3, 2019, from BrainyQuote.com: https://www.brainyquote.com/quotes/alfred_p_sloan_194032

21. Diagnosis. *Merriam-Webster.com*. Retrieved May 10, 2019, from https://www.merriam-webster.com/dictionary/diagnosis#medicalDictionary

22. Differential Diagnosis. *Wikipedia*. Retrieved June 1, 2019, from https://en.wikipedia.org/wiki/Differential_diagnosis#References

23. Differential Diagnosis. *Merriam-Webster.com*. Retrieved June 1, 2019, from https://www.merriam-webster.com/dictionary/differential%20diagnosis

24. Skinner, B. F. (1965). *Science and Human Behavior*. New York: Macmillan.

25. Chandon, P., Smith, R., Morowitz, V., Spangenberg, E. & Sprott, D. (2011). When does the past repeat itself? The interplay of behavior prediction and personal norms. *Journal of Consumer Behavior, 38,* 420-430.

26. Webb, Thomas, L. & Sheeran, P. (2006). Does changing behavioral intentions engender behavior change? A meta-analysis of the experimental evidence. *Psychological Bulletin, 132,* 249-268.

27. National Academies of Sciences, Engineering, and Medicine. (2015). *Improving Diagnosis in Heal Care*. Washington, DC: The National Academies Press. https://doi.org/10.17226/21794

28. American Psychiatric Association: Diagnostic and Statistical Manual of Mental Disorders: Diagnostic and Statistical Manual of Mental Disorders, Fifth Edition. Arlington, VA: American Psychiatric Association, 2013.

29. Air Traffic Controller Duties and Requirements. Retrieved April 26, 2019, from

https://study.com/articles/Air_Traffic_Controller_Salary_Dut
ies_and_Requirements.html

30. U.S. Department of Transportation, Federal Aviation
    Administration. (1995). Aeronautical information manual:
    official guide to basic flight information and ATC
    procedures. [Washington, D.C.]: Federal Aviation
    Administration: [For sale by the Supt. of Docs., U.S.
    G.P.O.].

31. U.S. Department of Transportation, Federal Aviation
    Administration. (2019). Aeronautical information manual:
    official guide to basic flight information and ATC
    procedures. [Washington, D.C.]: Federal Aviation
    Administration: [For sale by the Supt. of Docs., U.S.
    G.P.O.].

32. National Research Council. 1997. *Flight to the Future:
    Human Factors in Air Traffic Control.* Washington, DC: The
    National Academies Press. https://doi.org/10.17226/5493.

33. Bailey, L. L., & Thompson, R. C. (2000). The effects of
    performance feedback on air traffic control team
    coordination: A simulation study. U.S. Department of
    Transportation, Federal Aviation Administration.

34. Live ATC. Retrieved April 26, 2019, from
    https://www.liveatc.net

35. Buehler, N. (2019). Economics of Owning a Small Plane. Retrieved March 26, 2019, from https://www.investopedia.com/articles/wealth-management/121415/economics-owning-small-plane.asp

36. World Health Organization (2019). Burn-out an "occupational phenomenon": International Classification of Diseases. Retrieved May 29, 2019, from https://www.who.int/mental_health/evidence/burn-out/en/

37. Roger Stone Quotes. (n.d.). BrainyQuote.com. Retrieved July 6, 2019, from BrainyQuote.com Web site: https://www.brainyquote.com/quotes/roger_stone_441796

38. Roger Stone Nixon Quote - https://www.nytimes.com/1994/04/28/opinion/nixon-on-clinton.html

39. Holiday, R. (2012). Trust me, I'm lying: the tactics and confessions of a media manipulator. New York: Portfolio.

40. Sides, J., Shaw., Grossmann, M., & Lipsitz, K. (2012). Campaigns & Elections: Rules, Reality, Strategy, Choice. W. W. Norton & Company.

41. McNamara, M. (2012). The Political Campaign Desk Reference: A guide for campaign managers, professionals and candidates running for office. 2nd ed. Outskirts Press. Denver, Colorado.

42. "Coca-Cola: Happiness starts with a smile." *YouTube*, 28 Sept. 2015, youtu.be/1veWBLpGa78.

43. "Zappos – Pay with a cupcake." *YouTube*, 12 July, 2016, https://youtu.be/RhLTcylw8rs

44. "Examples of Experiential Marketing – Disha Kanchan." *YouTube*, 14 Sept, 2014, https://youtu.be/qZhbmlbfG5U

45. The History of Si Se Puede Retrieved May 1, 2019, from: https://ufw.org/research/history/history-si-se-puede/

46. Dangremond, S. (2018). Who Was the First Politician to Use "Make America Great Again" Anyway? Retrieved May 6, 2019, from https://www.townandcountrymag.com/society/politics/a25053571/donald-trump-make-america-great-again-slogan-origin/

47. "Then and Now: Ronald Reagan's Campaign Slogan was "Make America Great Again"?! (Season 1) | Bravo" *YouTube*, Retrieved May 28, 2019, from: https://www.youtube.com/watch?v=1zqKXg3CVzw

48. Wong, B. (2015). Types of Lawyers. LegalZoom, Retrieved June 10, 2019, from: https://www.legalzoom.com/articles/types-of-lawyers

49. Turner, T. L., (2015). Flexible IRAC: A Best Practices Guide. Southwestern Law School Research, 2015-16. SSRN:

https://ssrn.com/abstract=2633667 or
http://dx.doi.org/10.2139/ssrn.2633667

50. The IRAC Formula. Law Nerds, Retrieved June 10, 2019, from:
http://www.lawnerds.com/guide/irac.html#TheIRACFormula

51. Kübler-Ross, E. (2005). On Grief and Grieving: Finding the Meaning of Grief Through the Five Stages of Loss, Simon & Schuster

ABOUT THE AUTHOR

Abraham M. Gutsioglou, Ph.D. is an author, speaker, professor, and international consultant. Dr. Gutsioglou is a change management expert specialized in revitalizing failing and challenging situations.

Over the years, he has helped companies and individuals approach problems and ideas in innovative ways. He has advised organizational leaders how to create and lead business transformation strategies, impacting thousands of employees around the world with a record of successful execution.

Dr. Gutsioglou has worked in various industries like, manufacturing, technology, finance, healthcare, and academia. He is viewed by clients as a trusted partner and known to build teams to scale impact, efficiency, and to turnaround failing situations.